Ms. Phyllis A. Gentzen
Apt. 212
1600 Petroglyph Point Dr.
Prescott, AZ 86301-6595

D1459689

THE
ROAD
UNSEEN

THE ROAD UNSEEN

Peter & Barbara Jenkins

Thomas Nelson Publishers
Nashville • Camden • New York

Published in Nashville, Tennessee, by Thomas Nelson, Inc. and distributed in Canada by Lawson Falle, Ltd., Cambridge, Ontario.

Printed in the United States of America.

ISBN 0-8407-5961-4

Contents

As a child I learned how to love from my parents, because they loved me and my brothers and sisters so totally. When I was young they introduced me to God and served as my example of Him until I became old enough to comprehend Him for myself. This book is dedicated to my beloved father and mother, Frederick and Mary Jenkins.

—PJ

I wish to dedicate this book to the memory of my beloved brother, James Edward Pennell, who died at the young age of thirty-seven in 1983. "Jimmy" will always be close in my heart and memory.

And, I wish to dedicate this book to my parents, Betty and Ernie Pennell, and to my only sister, Vicky. I love you all with an everlasting love.

—BJJ

Acknowledgments

I f God were not such a real presence in our lives, there
would be no book called, *The Road Unseen*. Thank You,
God, for making Yourself so accessible to us and to everyone.

Also, without persistent inspiration from friends and
family, this book would not have been written. Thanks to
Jim Dobson for his compelling wisdom and sacrificial friendship. I deeply respect our other publisher, William Morrow,
for understanding our serious commitment to God and its
need for public expression: Pat, Larry, Sherri, Al, and
friends—the older I get, the wiser y'all get.

For further inspiration thanks to Welch and Gina Hill,
Bill and Camille Morris, Robert George, Calvin Scott, Tim
Scott, John and Patti Thompson, Ron and Cathy Hall, Mike
Blanton and Dan Harrell, Rita Jorgensen, Jerry Falwell,
Homer Kelly and our church family, M.C. and Margaret
Jenkins, Phil Yancey, Len LeSourd, John and Tibby Sherrill,
our friends at Word, Marilyn Jensen, Rev. Charles Green and
friends at the Word of Faith, Doug Denbow, Bob Sullivan,
Aubrey Harwell, Martha Smith and our many friends in the

book-selling business. Bruce and Lawanna McIver, you two are terrific. "Ain't no one going to fit me into a box!"

Special heartfelt thanks to my friends who work with me in our funky green and white trailer. They've inspired me, informed me, kept me reined in, prayed for me, and much more. Wally Hebert, you're extra special. So are you, Terri Baker, Tracy Smith, Judy Roberson, and Mary Margaret Reed. Okay, Swat Team, let's go to the top of the BSL, this time and many more!

A special note of appreciation to my loving brothers and sisters: Winky, Scott, Freddy, Betsy, and Abbi. Thanks Scott for your unwavering Christian commitment to our family. You're a great inspiration to me. A family that sticks together no matter what, stays together.

Thanks, Thomas Nelson, publishers of this book, you've done everything you said you'd do and much more. Publishing with you is more than business, it's family. Bob and Bobbie Wolgemuth, you mean so much to us, and the same goes for Mike and Gail Hyatt, who are even our neighbors. Watch out for those unidentified objects in your yard! Bruce Nygren, you've done a masterful job helping to make this book what it is, and we are proud to call you friend. Special thanks also to Sam Moore (the driving force), Lori Quinn, Joanie Boyle, Jahn Lutz, Sara Fortenberry, Victor Oliver, and the committed and hard-driving sales force at Nelson. You people, you "young turks," you're hot and climbing fast!

Barbara, honey, your gift to write is evident here. I'm so proud of what you've done, and I thank God for you. Love, Peter. Rebekah, Jed, and Luke, I pray you understand that your daddy must work long and late hours when he's writing a book. Your constant and sweet love lifts me as only a son or daughter's love can.

Above all, thanks to our readers. We hope that something we've written will enrich your life as the experience of it has enriched ours. We thank you for enthusiastically accepting our writing so that we can continue to live our wonderful lifestyle. The thousands of you who have written us encouraging, insightful, intellectually stimulating, critical, and loving letters, thanks. Your concern lifts us over the bumps and blahs of life and keeps us keepin' on. All our books are for you.

—PJ

Writing is tough. As the mother of three small children, there is little time left over to rest, read, and relax—much less write a book. Without the faithful help of Dot Murphy and Zephyr Fite, I never could have written my part of this book. They stepped in and rocked my babies, washed dishes and clothes, and kept my house in order while I labored over the words you are about to read.

I would like to thank the women in my weekly Bible study who have become my good friends and prayer partners in daily life. They have given me their support, and for their faithful friendship I am grateful. Don't be embarrassed girls, here goes: Judy Ide, Ann Purdy, Lisa Carr, Doris Prince, Brenda Hebert, Linda Couser, Carol High, Gail Hyatt, Gloria Merritt, Karen Costello, and Lynn Haas.

I wish to thank God for giving me the ability to put words on paper and have them make sense. He is the ultimate Creator and His glory cannot be shared.

And, for the guidance from our editor on this book, Bruce Nygren, I wish to say how pleased I am with his input. His meticulous care over every sentence showed me how to focus my thoughts and dig out the best meaning. Thank you, Bruce.

And, I'd like to thank Pat Golbitz, our previous editor, (*The Walk West*), who was the first to tell me I could write. Without you, Pat, I might never have had the courage to write a word. See what your encouragement has done!

Finally, I wish to thank my friend, joint heir/partner, and husband, Peter. He has always given me the freedom to be myself, to use the gifts God has given me without feeling threatened. Without his guidance, protection, and covering, I would never have walked across America, nor had a story to tell or a book to write. With deep respect and appreciation, I wish to say thank you, Peter.

—BJJ

1

The Road Unseen

Peter

"I was on a slow train crossing China. Three uniformed men rushed by me, down a narrow hallway. In the next car I heard people arguing loudly. They were shouting in high-pitched, Oriental voices. Their words came fast and the tone was sharply grating. What were these three anxious men looking for? Were they members of some branch of the Chinese secret police? Could they be on special assignment, the object of their search "a foreigner with a red beard and blondish hair, dressed in blue jeans and a T-shirt that said, *The Walk West*"? Were they after me?

The narrow coach rocked and creaked as I lay on my bunk, dazed from the more than twelve hours that had passed since I'd boarded this train the night before in the city of Xi'an. In the train station I'd felt as if I were being swept away by a flooding river of people. I rolled onto my stomach, trying to get a better view down the hall where the "agents" had just disappeared. I was headed for Inner Mongolia. It was summertime, 1984.

My feet hung out of the short bunk, and the very used

wool blanket I'd been issued barely covered me. The shouting quieted and I glanced out at the eroded and barren countryside moving past so rhythmically. The windows had no curtains and were streaked with dust and finger prints. The floor was yellowed with age, clean but dull, faded by hundreds of moppings with nothing but cold water. Hot water cost money in China, and so did floor-cleaning detergent. On the legs of the bunks were the strands of many mops.

If they were searching for me, how could these agents have missed me? I was the only non-Chinese passenger on this train that was packed tighter than any public transportation I'd ever been on, including the New York subway. In fact, here in super-jammed China, I often found myself yearning for the "open spaces" of New York City, the same way I yearned for the mountain valleys of the Rockies when trapped in rush-hour traffic in Los Angeles.

My bunk was in a semiprivate sleeping room that was really no room at all. It had no door and had just the slimmest aisle dividing three pairs of very narrow, hard bunks. These bunks, called "hard sleepers" for good reason, were very expensive for the average Chinese, and yet unbelievably cheap to me, a "rich" American. The ticket for a journey of hundreds of miles had cost just thirteen dollars.

Most of the Chinese sat on hard seats, three and four across, even if their train ride was for thousands of miles and lasted five days—from the oil fields of Xinjiang Province by the Russian border to a fishing village south of Shanghai on the western coast.

Everything seemed hard in China, from backbreaking work to what one sat or slept on. There was very little luxury here, luxury that almost every American considered an absolute necessity—like cushions on a chair, refrigerated soft drinks, or personal cars.

The sounds of running feet interrupted my thoughts. The police, or whoever they were, were coming back toward my bunk! The men ran through the door at the end of my car pushing their way through a family that was blocking the hall. The family was drinking tea from two old glass jars and eating a few unbaked rolls. Normally, the sight of someone eating these raw rolls made me nauseated, but I was too worried by the three men to be bothered.

The agitated trio rushed by my bunk like hunting dogs hot on a fresh trail. This time they went to the end of the sleeping car and began systematically searching all the bunk rooms. I had no idea what they were shouting in their piercing Chinese, but I imagined them shrieking, "Get up! Hurry! DO NOT DELAY!"

For all I knew they were announcing a new revolution and were about to stop the train and make us go back to Beijing. Or maybe they were searching for a suspected spy. The more I learned of how the Chinese government operated the more insecure and paranoid I became.

The officers took about ten minutes to question the people in the bunk room two slots down the hall. By now a crowd was gathering, as the Chinese love to gather around a happening like this. Everyone seemed to be wearing dark blue clothing. There were many soldiers on this train, and they wore undecorated army-green uniforms with matching cloth hats adorned only by one red, five pointed star—the symbol of their beloved motherland.

Then the investigators were questioning the people in the room next door. Their voices got louder. I was tempted to jump down and move, but I knew there was no place to hide, especially looking the way I did. Maybe when they got to our room they wouldn't see me since I was on the top bunk, so close to the ceiling I couldn't put my knees up. I began to go over all the things I'd done the past month since I'd arrived in China.

In this land of a million secrets, and a billion eyes trying to make sure there were no secrets, I had immediately learned that everywhere I went I was being watched. I had been taking pictures constantly, wanting to capture the first-time intensity of everything in this world I'd only imagined and dreamed about before. Had I taken pictures of some forbidden factory down some off-limits alley in Beijing or snapped a portrait of some person with a secret identity while bicycling around Chengdu? Could the slides I had taken of that military-looking group of low buildings in a secluded mountain pass in Tibet have been a secret missile site?

Were they after my cameras? Would they take all my film? I was thankful I'd already sent home the fifty rolls I'd taken in Tibet and around Mt. Everest. What if they didn't know the difference between exposed film and unexposed film? They might take all my film, and then I would have none in Mongolia and wherever else in China this adventure would take me.

The shouting stopped. I sneaked a look and saw the sweaty faces of the agents peering into the room. All Chinese people no longer looked alike to me. The tallest of the three had a broad face, narrow eyes that slanted down, and a very muscular build. He looked Mongolian and when he spoke, his voice was almost soothing.

The shortest of the three began asking questions of the people in the lower bunks. He seemed to be an officer and was obviously upset. As he began to shriek a string of questions, I moved closer to the wall hoping that if he hadn't seen me, he wouldn't.

The Chinese men acted as if they could no longer stand not finding out the information they were seeking. I wondered if they would resort to violence to get whatever they were looking for. Then, for no apparent reason, the Chinese version of Musak began pouring loudly out of every speaker in the train. The music sounded familiar, for it seemed that every public place in China played the same tape. The sounds of this high-pitched music further enraged the men because they could no longer interrogate anyone. They began shouting to each other and rushed off. I figured they were headed to tell the conductor or whoever was responsible that they couldn't possibly carry on their investigation over that shrill stuff.

I stayed pressed against the wall for about ten minutes, my anxiety building. Exhausted from the tension of the search and my long, long hours crammed into the train, I finally closed my eyes on the dusty hills and eroded vastness of central China slipping by my window. The constant clicking sounds of the wheels on the tracks lulled me into a trancelike calm until the train roared through an especially narrow, dark tunnel. I opened my eyes and realized I was far too excited to fall asleep. Were those agents going to come back? Had they found their "man"?

My mind raced from one thing to another until I fixed my eyes again on the countryside. The passing scenes and movements eventually calmed me. I saw oxen breaking ground far up on a hillside and women cutting hay by hand. There were blurred views of donkey carts loaded to overflowing with firewood, headed down narrow dirt lanes. I did a double take when I saw a man pulling a small plow while a woman held it straight as they cultivated their commune's corn. It was like watching a movie that had been shot on another planet.

Where was my notebook? I wanted to record what had just happened. But before I could write anything down I was surprisingly overwhelmed by strong feelings of homesickness. I couldn't get my family, my farm, and my country off my mind. Here I was at the opposite end of the world feeling desperately lonely, and there was no way to go home except in my mind.

Not only was I as many miles as I could possibly be from where I belonged, but I felt I was a billion people away from everything I believed in. Here I saw the opposite—the tremendous lack of freedom, the all pervasive Communism, the stifling limitations on personal initiative...And, there were no Mexican food places! My walk across America had introduced me to our incredible USA, but being in China made my extraordinary country come into focus like never before.

The three officers never did return to question me. I learned later that they had been looking for a stolen purse, not a bearded American "spy." The night came to China, and hours passed as I thought about my life and my place in this world. I wanted to pray, to ask God to take away these swarming feelings of insecurity and loneliness. I knew I didn't need someone else to pray with, but I wanted someone to be with me just the same. I knew there were Christians in China, maybe even one in my bunk room, but they either couldn't speak English or wouldn't talk about religion with a foreigner.

When I was at home I never worried about being too far away from my kind of people and my friends and family. They were everywhere. Now they were nowhere. It was just me and a couple of snapshots of Barbara and the kids, a picture of my horse, Shocker, and my memories. Finally, I began to write in my notebook. I realized I didn't want to write about this latest adventure of mine with the searching Chinese agents after all. Instead I felt compelled to write down all the things that mattered to me most.

I wrote how I missed the wilderness and hamburgers. I missed my king-size bed and driving fast on a country road. I wished for air conditioning and longed to hear my pastor's sermons. I wanted to go anywhere where everyone spoke English, and I wanted to watch "The David Letterman Show" or "Monday Night Football." I craved ice cold spring water and the freedom I felt in the USA. I wanted just to be in the same room with Barbara, Rebekah, and Jed.

And I wrote down that I really missed God. I didn't expect Him to come and sit down beside me, but I missed what He was in my life. He was my ultimate security. He was my guide through life and my main source of discipline. He was my friend, more faithful than any person, the most faithful presence on earth. He was profound wisdom and pure love. I yearned for His arms of love to hold me. But He seemed so far away.

I knew He was here, but I felt so lonely just the same. And there was no one around to fellowship with. Lying on that bunk I realized more clearly than ever before how important my relationship with God was. I decided right there, on that slow train across China, that when I got back home Barbara and I would finally write a book about our road unseen, our walk with God.

Barbara and I are known publicly for the roads we've traveled down while walking across America, and yet we've never fully told the stories from our most profound adventure, our walk as Christians. Millions of people who have read our books, *A Walk Across America*, and *The Walk West*, think the incidents told there were the whole story. But in almost every adventure, in almost every life-changing event, there was an unseen road, the story of how our relationship with God played a crucial role. We'd like to tell you those stories as well as tell you about some of the adventures we've had with Him since our walk across America ended.

We've had incredible adventures in the physical world, like paddling through swamps at night looking for huge alligators. We've crossed the Rocky Mountains and staggered, crazed by the blistering sun, through the western deserts. I've watched killer whales circle a salmon fishing boat I worked on in the wild waters of Alaska, not to mention all that happened to me in China (the subject of my next book). None of these experiences, though, has had as significant an impact as our road unseen.

Barbara and I have had adventures that left our hearts soaring or crunched. Our minds have been constantly challenged as we've learned of different peoples and philosophies until we thought we could hold no more. And yet we are not just people with physical bodies burning for adventure and hearts and minds always ready for challenges. We are people with spirits and souls that yearn for more of the adventure that is our relationship with God. Come along with us down these unseen roads.

2

The Call

"Hi! Honey!" Peter shouted above the static in the radio phone from somewhere in the middle of the Gulf of Mexico. "How's my country girl? Did you get my last letter? How's everything there in the apartment?"

The phone shrieked and buzzed, and Peter's questions came so fast I couldn't answer them. Our voices were covering hundreds of miles, and I feared we would be cut off at any moment.

"Everything's great," I yelled back into the phone, hoping that my true emotions were not showing in the tone of my voice. I was a lonely new bride living in New Orleans while Peter worked on an off-shore oil rig, one week out and one week at home with me in our first apartment.

"Honey, you wouldn't believe the gigantic fish I caught today; set an all time record. It was so big we had to hoist it up with a crane—weighed sixty-eight pounds. I'll bring some fillets when I come home in two days."

The static started again. It was so loud I had to pull the phone away from my ear. My feelings hurt as much as my ear. How could Peter be having so much fun while I sat here in this little apartment, all alone? We had only been married two months.

"Barbara, can you hear me?"

Shriek—wr-r-r-r—buzz-z-z-z——click.

The radio phone went dead. I swallowed hard and fought back the tears. I needed Peter right now, desperately, and he was somewhere off the coast of New Orleans...fishing.

I gently put down the receiver. I felt cheated. Here I was, just married, and my life was not the way it was supposed to be. Newlyweds were supposed to go on honeymoons and spend endless hours in romantic settings and moods. They were supposed to have candlelit dinners, leisurely strolls, soft music, and lots of tender love and affection. Brides and grooms were supposed to be so wrapped up in their love that all the world stood still. That wasn't true for me. Peter was gone on another of his adventures, and we would be leaving soon to finish Peter's walk across America—at least three thousand miles on foot. What a honeymoon.

This all seemed like a dream, sometimes good and sometimes bad. The good part of the dream was Peter, my beloved, my new husband, the man I had prayed for and had waited for so many years. It was fascinating, thinking back over the past year and remembering how we had met and fallen in love and how my life had changed drastically.

Peter Gorton Jenkins was a very magnetic person, and he enchanted me more than anyone else I had met in my twenty-seven years—and I certainly had known other men who were interesting. But he was the crazy man everyone was talking about on campus, the one who had been converted to Christ at a revival meeting, the one who was walking across America and writing a story for *National Geographic* magazine. When we met in March, 1975, at The

New Orleans Baptist Theological Seminary, Peter had already walked from upstate New York down to New Orleans. Just two months earlier, I had begun study for a master's in religious education after working as a social worker for three years in Mississippi.

Not long after Peter came to the seminary, the students were hosting a student-faculty party in the women's dormitory. Peter, who had come as the guest of a faculty member, stood out like a flashing neon light in the crowd of freshly shaven, cologne-splashed preacher men. His carrot-red beard and long blond hair contributed to an unkempt look. While dozens of the male students were wearing dress pants, tailored shirts, and polished shoes, Peter wore a pair of faded brown corduroys, a blue plaid shirt, and sneakers with holes in them.

But it wasn't just his clothes and grooming that set him apart. His whole presence was foreign and a bit different. There was something unprogrammed about him and he had a faraway look in his eyes. He certainly didn't appear to be a Baptist. He didn't seem to be a religious man of any type, for that matter. He reminded me of an owl, quietly looking from side to side, trying to figure out what was going on in this group of Bible students.

I was intrigued by him immediately. I liked his round, questioning eyes. They were blue and clear, wide open like windows through which I could see far inside. After everyone had gone through the buffet line, I made my way over to the group of professors where Peter was seated. I could feel his eyes watching me. I sat down in a chair next to him and chatted with one of the professors until someone introduced us. It was a polite introduction, and I quickly went on my way. But I knew Peter Jenkins was someone special, and I wanted to find out why.

Weeks passed. On a warm, lazy Saturday afternoon in June, a water fight broke out in my dormitory between some of the women students working in the kitchen. Some young men who were visiting in the T.V. lounge joined in, and before long water was flying in every direction like an afternoon thunderstorm. Pitcher after pitcher was filled and dumped, and the floors were soon covered with puddles from the front hall to the kitchen. At the peak of the battle, I was chasing a preacher friend, a full pitcher in hand, when the front door opened and in walked the red-bearded stranger. I took one look at Peter Jenkins and upended the whole pitcher on his head.

I turned quickly and ran the other way, my instincts telling me he would not let me get by with such a thing. I was right. Peter charged like a bull, picked me up, threw me over his shoulder, and headed for the kitchen. A fresh bucket of homemade ice cream was waiting on a counter, and Peter dipped his hand in the metal container and rubbed vanilla ice cream all over my face and hair. I screamed and laughed and ordered him to put me down.

From that moment on we were together every possible minute—between classes, after lunch, at night before the women's dorm was locked—and we walked hand in hand around the seventy-five acre campus. This unusual, wild, captivating man was winning my heart.

New Orleans in early summer was a perfect city for romance. Every tree, every bush, every flower burst with beauty and dripped with humidity, making the plants and flowers grow so fast no one could hedge them in. Our love was like that. It bloomed and grew and vibrated. The sultry weather enriched our lips with warmth and our touches with fire. We talked endlessly about each other, our opposite backgrounds, our dreams, and our fast-growing love. Neither of us could explain the force that pulled us like the current of a mighty river. We didn't care. We had both found that special person who filled the gap inside.

The summer passed without us. In a world of our own we were not interested in sunbathing by the lake with our friends or hanging out at the Café du Monde in the French Quarter. We wanted only to be alone, to fall deeper and deeper in love. We walked on clouds, above everyone else, far away from the troubles of the world. Our kisses grew longer and sweeter. Our embraces became harder and harder to unlock.

One fall afternoon in November, Peter and I were walking across campus when a gust of wind blasted our faces. This was hurricane season, and New Orleans was in the direct path of a storm, now only hours away. We were arguing and our voices grew stronger and louder with the wind. We often had "debates" but this time our argument was not about politics or religion but about our future together. We had reached a point in our romance where we either had to get married or call it quits. I thought I wanted to marry Peter, but I did not want to join him on the rest of his walk across America.

"Believe me, we are supposed to get married and you are supposed to come with me," Peter announced. He sounded authoritative and commanding. "God has shown me this is what you are supposed to do!"

I didn't believe him, and I certainly didn't like his telling me what I was supposed to do. And was he throwing God in as a way to convince me to go with him?

My insides whirled like the blowing winds. Who did he think he was, this wayfarer, this wanderer who had been a born-again Christian for only six months and could not even quote John 3:16? Who did this babe in Christ think he was, telling me, an old hand at the Bible and Christianity, that God had shown him I was supposed to walk across America with him?

He was expecting me to fold up and leave everything behind, the rest of my education and the secure future I could have after seminary. How could he ask me to give up clean clothes, jewelry, a bed, my friends, television, shopping, a car, a steady income—everything known to modern woman?

Peter Jenkins had nothing to offer me—no money, no job, no home, nothing except three thousand miles of sweat and blisters while walking across this country. All Peter did have were his dreams and adventures. This was the age of women's liberation, and the idea of laying aside my personal goals and taking off with this vagabond was like stepping back into the dark ages.

But Peter would not give up. "God gave me a vision and showed me that you are meant to come with me," he said.

A vision? This really was the last straw! I couldn't stand it any longer. Since when did God give anyone in today's world a vision? He had certainly never given me one, nor had I ever heard a voice or had a dream or any of those other-world things. My love for Peter was real, but this was ridiculous.

"Why don't you finish your walk across America by yourself? I'll drive out to meet you along the way, then come and join you when you reach the end. Now! Doesn't that sound like a good idea, the logical thing to do?" I said to Peter.

"That will never work. You have to walk. It's the only way!" No amount of pleading, arguing, or even tears would change his thinking. Nothing would budge him from finishing his walk, and marriage meant that I would have to go with him.

"I've made up my mind," I finally told him. "I don't want to see you or be around you anymore until I know what to do. In two weeks let's go to church together one last time, and if something doesn't happen, if I don't get a sense of direction, then it's over. I mean it. I cannot go on like this."

I needed relief from the internal pressure; the two weeks would give me time to rest, think, and pray. My friends were giving me advice, and some of my professors were encouraging me to forget about Peter and finish my education. Voices jabbered at me from every side, and my thoughts were jumbled. I felt caught, as though I were tangled in a net and couldn't fight my way out. My heart told me that Peter was right for me, but in my mind, the circumstances, the timing of our relationship were all wrong. Marrying Peter meant turning my whole life and world upside down and inside out.

Saturday night...late. The final night before Peter and I were to go to church together. He had tried to see me several times during the two-week separation, but I had refused.

My dormitory room was just down the hall from the little chapel on the second floor of William Carey Hall. Most of the women were already back from their dates, asleep, or taking a shower. I tiptoed into the chapel, sure that no one had seen me. I didn't want any company. I didn't want anyone telling me what I should or should not do.

On my knees I began to pray, not timidly, but with boldness and determination. If I had ever needed to hear from God, it was now. No more games. No more playing with Scriptures and theorizing. I needed help, and I was going to take hold of heaven and not let go until God answered me. For a long time I lay on the floor, asking God to hear my plea. Was it possible? Was I really supposed to go with Peter as his wife? Or, hopefully, was Peter to quit his walk and settle down with me so I could finish my degree in religious education? Then we could get secure jobs. Maybe Peter would even become a student and turn into a preacher. Oh, dear God, what?

Several hours passed. A faint light began to shine through the chapel windows. In only a short while Peter and I would go to church one last time together. I might never see Peter again. If it turned out that way, I was ready. I had no more energy to struggle with him, to argue about his walk. I just wanted to get dressed, to go to church, and to end this agonizing ordeal.

Word of Faith Temple on Read Road was packed with more than one thousand people. Arriving at the last minute, Peter and I had to be ushered to the front row to the only two adjoining seats left in the entire building. I was tired and didn't care where we sat. Besides, I didn't know many people in the church anyway, and they didn't know me or my special problem on this Sunday, November 16, 1975.

I had chosen to take Peter to this nondenominational church because they were tolerant of blue jeans, sneakers, and unconventional dress. And I did like their freedom of worship, their emotion and excitement. Although I was a Baptist I enjoyed different churches and forms of worship. I knew Peter would fit right in and savor the experience of this church, just as he did every other adventure in his life. And no one would notice the holes in his shoes. The service began.

"We have no idea what God is going to dig out from here today," said the special speaker for the day, an elderly woman everyone called "Mom Beall." She was in her eighties and spoke from a wheel chair. I had never heard a woman minister before.

Now, there's a woman who has her act together, I thought. *She must be important, speaking to this big church, especially since few women ever get to give sermons. I bet she never dreamed of doing a crazy thing like what Peter is asking me to do. She looks so spiritual. She sounds so well-informed about the Bible, and she probably has a long life of experiences to draw from, making her strong and wise. I'm sure, now, this is the end for Peter and me.*

"I'm glad to be here," Mom Beall continued. "You know, it's thirty degrees in Detroit, where I'm from, and snowing. So I'm glad to be here, where the Spirit of the Lord is! I believe there is a reason for my being here." Her voice was soft, low, and inviting. "I would like to have you turn today, please, to the twenty-fourth chapter of the book of Genesis. I'll begin with the forty-second verse.

And I came this day unto the well, and said, O LORD
God of my master Abraham, if now thou do prosper my
way which I go: Behold, I stand by the well of water;
and it shall come to pass, that when the virgin cometh
forth to draw water, and I say to her, Give me, I pray
thee, a little water of thy pitcher to drink; and she say to
me, Both drink thou, and I will also draw for thy cam-
els: let the same be the woman whom the LORD hath ap-
pointed out for my master's son. And before I had done
speaking in mine heart, Rebekah came forth with her
pitcher on her shoulder; and she went down unto the
well and drew water. (KJV)

Mom Beall read on, and I struggled to keep my mind
focused on this familiar Bible story. In some ways, I envied
those Old Testament folk. God seemed so often to give them
signs or just tell them what to do. Why did His plans for me
have to be so mysterious?

"...And he said unto them, Hinder me not, seeing the
LORD hath prospered my way; send me away that I may go to
my master." Mom Beall's voice was growing louder and more
animated. "We will call the damsel, and inquire at her
mouth. And they called Rebekah, and said unto her, Wilt
thou go with this man? And she said, I will go.

Mom Beall lifted her old eyes from the Bible and said,
"May God bless the reading of His Word. My text is found in
the fifty-eighth verse." She paused, then said in nearly a
whisper, halting after each word, "Will...You...Go-
...With...This...Man?" The words ricocheted through my
mind. Her soft voice penetrated like a needle. She repeated
the words again, taking even longer this time, drawing each
word out like pulling pails of water from a deep well: "Will
...You...Go...With...This...Man?"

The aged woman then began to pray, pleading as I had
never heard anyone before. She asked God to meet the needs
of the people and to speak to every waiting heart.

Her prayer completed, Mom Beall retold the romantic story of the search for a wife for Isaac, Abraham's only son. She compared it to the search that God was making for people who would hear God's voice, respond to His call, and go with Him. She said His call gave each person the chance to say yes or no, but like Rebekah, it would mean leaving everything behind, going to a land or lifestyle totally different from before, and trusting God to lead him through the unknown.

I went into a mental lapse, not believing what I was hearing. My brain rebelled. My body tightened. Mom Beall groaned repeatedly, her old voice heavy with longing, "Oh, will you go with this man?"

I thought I might die on the spot and shrank lower and lower into my cushioned seat, almost sliding onto the floor. I didn't dare look at Peter. Out of the corner of my eye I could see he was squaring his shoulders, puffing up like a rooster ready to crow. After breaking up with Peter, giving him one last chance, praying all night in my dorm, asking God for a sign—this just couldn't be happening.

Mom Beall laughed. "What romance! He's a wonderful God. He makes something out of nothing. And Rebekah said, 'I...Will...Go.' " Mom Beall's voice now thundered, echoing through the loudspeakers, off the walls, from the ceiling, up from the carpeted floors. There was no escape. I knew God was speaking to me. This was too bizarre to be a coincidence, too timely to be a fluke, too piercing to ignore. God's voice was calling me.

I leaned over and whispered in Peter's ear, "I will go with you."

The sermon ended. All I wanted to do was fade away, get out, and not look back. Something incredible had just taken place, but once I had escaped, I would reason the whole thing out...maybe even reason it away.

Mom Beall was rolled away from the podium, and the

pastor of the church, Reverend Charles Green, took the microphone. The organ began to play softly in the background, and the pastor lifted his head high and looked toward heaven. The smile on his face was as broad as the Bible he clutched to his chest. He began to sing, "Where he leads me I will follow...I'll go with Him, with Him, all the way."

3

Tuned to the Truth

Peter

I felt like I was soaring about fifty feet off the floor, experiencing the highest of highs, and I never wanted to come back to earth. It was March of 1975.

A middle-aged woman named Mary walked up to me and said, "Did you know that there are angels in heaven singing for you, right now?" The thought that angels were singing just for me was certainly a beautiful one, but I was so overwhelmed by the rushes of purity I was already experiencing I didn't really concentrate on it.

Only ten minutes earlier I'd decided to become a Christian, during a revival meeting's "altar call." Here I was in the depths of the Bible-belt, having come to the large meeting to take pictures. I'd never been anywhere near a revival, so I'd come out of curiosity. In fact, the only time I'd ever heard the word *revival* used was in college when we studied Greek *Revival* architecture.

Strangers walked up to me, grabbed my hand, and said things like, "Thank God, young man, you've decided to follow the Lord." "Doesn't it feel great to be born again?"

31

"You've just made the wisest decision of your life." One man, dressed in polyester-blend pants and a windbreaker that said *Auto Mart* on it, heard my Yankee accent and said, "Well, good. Another Yankee's gotten himself right with God."

At first, walking through the South on my way across America had been like being in a different country. I had culture shock. But now I was used to the way southerners "tawked," ate different foods like "boiled okry," and remembered the Civil War as though it had ended last year. I had become used to their more gentle pace of life and now preferred it to the more "hyper" speed of Northern living. "Northern" meant any place in America that might have sent soldiers to fight against the South.

But here at the revival I didn't understand all that these people were saying about what had just happened between God and me. "Born again"..."Saved"..."The Lord led you here tonight"..."Praise the Lord"..."Well God finally's got you away from the Devil"..."Ain't God good"—these words seemed as normal in their vocabulary as "taxes," "commute," and "weekend" were to my family and friends in New York and Connecticut.

Then Mary came back to tell me something. She was slim, over forty, and dressed more fashionably than most of the other ten thousand people present. She stared at me with probing eyes, trying to figure out what I was feeling and thinking. I remembered what she'd said about the angels singing because I'd become a Christian. I wondered what kind of songs they sang. *Wouldn't that be a great "live" concert to have on cassette*, I thought.

"Peter, this great elation that you're feeling now..." she paused. "You *are* feeling great elation, aren't you?"

"Yes," I said.

She continued. Her voice was soft and I strained to hear. "At this moment it may seem like these great feelings are going to last forever, but they won't. Being a Christian is not based on feelings. You're on a mountain top now, but someday, sooner or later, you'll be far away from these great feelings. You may even wonder if all this ever happened."

A few of the people standing around me made faces like they disapproved of what she was saying.

"Your Christian walk is based on faith, not feelings."

I was so thrilled that there could be good feelings mixed in with faith that I really didn't care about her opinions. It was like I'd just graduated from high school and someone had said, "Did you know that someday you'll be a mature adult and won't feel as excited about life anymore?"

Well, more than ten years have passed since my conversion in Mobile, Alabama. Mary was right—I was on a mountain top that night, my spiritual Mt. Everest. The feelings lasted a long time, but that mountain top hasn't lasted all these years. Maybe I've been on more mountain tops than some, but I've also climbed, sometimes crawled, out of some awfully steep valleys, too.

Ten years ago I became one of God's children. God has millions and millions of children, but I feel like He knows my needs and my heart as if I were His only child. It makes me realize how vastly incredible the LORD is. He's so much more than wonderful. He's more mighty than one million of man's most powerful computers, and yet He has the capacity to feel our joy and pain as deeply as a billion hearts. He has changed everything for me.

Please come with me, back in time ten years, as I take you to the night I met God.

My expectations of what to expect at a revival were vague and fuzzy. I knew little about this sort of thing, but picked up my pace to get there before it started. The closer I came, the more I looked around for the striped tent of my preconceptions, but saw only an auditorium, like a small Superdome. The parking lots were filled with hundreds and hundreds of cars. Most seemed new or at least well polished. Surely all these cars weren't here for the revival; there must be a rock concert inside the auditorium. No tent was anywhere in sight, so I went around back; it wasn't there either. Maybe I had misunderstood the dates on the billboard, but I thought that I would check the auditorium to see what was happening, anyway. Inside, I heard singing. To my amazement, the whole place was full, and a huge choir was singing a hymn. At least ten thousand people filled the place, and I stood there wondering where I could sit.

The thousands of seats stopped about a hundred feet before the elevated stage, so I took a deep breath, worked up my courage and headed for the empty space below the stage, on the floor. I could take some good pictures this close, and be in the middle of the action, too. After the choir was seated, a man dressed in a classy tan suit approached the microphone and started to sing a solo. His voice was as clear as the air at fifteen thousand feet and as soothing as a father's arm. I felt more comfortable behind my black Nikon camera with its long lens as I sat in front of all these people. A row of clergymen sat behind the singer, some of them staring at me as I crouched on the floor. I was too excited about getting emotion-packed pictures to wonder why I was there. I calmly clicked the shutter again and again, feeling hip and smug.

The singer, John McKay, finished his solo, then a woman in a long flowing gown came to sing. Her hair was as shiny and radiant as her face. I sat on the floor with my legs crossed and kept pushing my long hair back out of my face to take more pictures. A tall man in his thirties charged from his seat at the back of the platform and rushed to a microphone like a Dallas Cowboy linebacker. I kept the telephoto lens to my face, and watched, and snapped. The lens made me feel protected and covered from this preacher's view.

The over six-foot-tall Texan looked as if he were ready to jolt some folks. With a battered Bible in his big hand, he went right to his message. His first words of the night were hushed.

"I'm not going to keep you long, but I want to talk to you tonight about God. I'm here to give you some good news. How well you listen could determine the rest of your life and your eternity." Before the ten thousand people, James Robison was quiet just long enough for that thought to take hold.

I didn't really believe all this nonsense about eternity, but I was more interested than I wanted to admit.

The audience became attentive as the sermon heated up and James shouted, "I want you people to know that repentance is required to know God. Repentance is a forgotten message in America today, but I'm not going to forget it because it's a Bible message! You have to repent to get right with God. You can be a Baptist and go to hell. A survey was taken at the Huntsville Penitentiary in Texas and 72 percent of the inmates were Baptist."

Laughter broke the tension. He yelled, "I don't care if you're a Methodist, I don't care if you're a Catholic, I don't care if you're a Presbyterian or Pentecostal, I don't care if you're a pastor or a seminary professor. I don't care what you are, friend. Salvation is not guaranteed just because you belong to a church."

Most of what he said about knowing God, repenting and salvation, I didn't clearly understand. But I knew I was at a place where something real and truth-tuned was happening. Mixed up, feeling self-conscious, I stayed on the floor, locked between the ten thousand people and the preacher. My camera was now dangling, ignored, and no longer hiding me from the preacher's eyes.

"I want you to know that most decisions for

church membership are no different than joining a civic club, or the country club, and that kind of membership is keeping people from knowing God. Just being a member of a church will not save you or change your life. You can quit drinking, quit drugs, quit running around on your wife, quit stealing, quit everything and join a church and still not repent. You can become a good person and still not get to God. If you enjoy life without God, you have never repented and you have never been born of God!"

James Robison paused and then walked from behind the white oak podium. He pointed toward the audience, but it seemed that he was pointing right at me. The sweat beaded on his reddened face and seemed to evaporate before my eyes from the heat of his preaching. He bent down, inches from the front of the stage.

"When I ask you tonight if you are a Christian, many of you will answer and say you joined a church." He practically screamed: "Joining a church won't make you a Christian any more than joining the Lion's Club will make you a lion!"

His words began to penetrate. "From the day you were born, you wanted to 'do your own thing' and you were rebellious against God. If you want to really know God, you've got to repent of this rebellion, which the Bible calls *sin*."

Like a diamond-tipped drill, the message pierced the hard and hidden layers of my personality. For no logical reason, I felt worse and more pulled apart than when my dog Coops died. I was dying right here on this empty floor. My life flashed before me as I felt a shining light expose my past twenty-two years.

James turned up his volume and the impact was increased. "Religion is not the answer! *Salvation is!* Salvation is committing your life to Jesus Christ and believing in Him. But don't think you are going to use Jesus for a passport to heaven. If you confess Him, you must believe He is God's only son Who was sent to die for your sins."

James wiped his forehead and paced across the platform. He cleared his throat, as if to tell us he was going to blast us with more. "I remember an evangelist who walked up to a man in the congregation one night, and the man had a big ol' frown on his face. He looked as if someone had stuck a prune in his mouth. The evangelist put his hand on the man's shoulder and asked him if he wanted to become a Christian. The man growled back at the evangelist, 'I'm a deacon in this church!' And the evangelist said, 'Don't let that stand in your way.' "

Most of the men in the auditorium laughed. James never stopped for the crowd's laughter but bore down harder. "It's possible to be a deacon, an elder, a steward, a Sunday school teacher, or go to church all your life and not know the Lord."

I was still full of doubt and cynicism. Something about this whole scene made me nervous and uncomfortable. As unexpected as death, embarrassing tears began to roll down my face. A gentle hand was wiping away something inside of me, something I wanted to hold on to. This Texan with his Bible message spoke respectfully of all those as deeply moved as me. His voice was soft and pleading.

"From every walk of life I've seen people give their lives to Jesus Christ, and tonight I'm going to ask many of you to come forward and say you will commit your life to Him. The reason I must ask you to come before all these people is because the Bible says that you must confess Jesus before men, if you want Him to confess you before the Father.

"All over the auditorium, I want everyone to bow their heads, every head bowed, every eye closed. I want you to listen prayerfully."

With all these thousands of men, women and

children, the place became as quiet as the deep woods. An awesome hush fell over everyone. I bowed my head, trying to pull myself together. "I want to ask you a question and I want you to tell me the truth. You be honest with God. You be honest with yourself. My question is *not*, Are you religious? It is *not*, Are you a church member? It is *not*, Are you a spiritual person?"

There was a long, silent break. This was my first revival and now the preacher was about to ask "the" question. I was deeply defensive and besides, I was just an observer, so why should I care what question he was about to ask. A sense of panic hit me. I was afraid for James Robison to ask his final question of the night. I was trying desperately to be rational yet I felt out of control and helpless. I had never been so moved. This was the last place on earth I expected such a thing to happen.

The powerful question finally came. "Have you ever repented of your sin and turned your life over to Jesus Christ? Are you saved?"

I was going to die. The deepest corners of my being were lit with thousand-watt bulbs. It was as if God Himself were looking into my soul, through all my excuses, my dark secrets. All of me was exposed in God's searchlight.

When the question ended its roaring echo, I decided for the first time to admit I needed God. This must be the God I had been searching for, and the same One they worshiped back in Murphy at Mt. Zion. The evangelist remained reverent and quiet for long seconds. Then, "All of you who want to come forward and accept Jesus Christ as your personal Savior, please raise your hands."

My back faced the thousands but I didn't care what anyone else did or thought. I knew I was ready. I lifted my hand toward heaven. The preacher then asked all of us with raised arms to come up front and pray publicly. Although I had raised my hand to God, a public prayer was something else. My overamped brains and self-will still fought against this decision that seemed so irrational. However, all I had to do was stand up since I was already by the platform. So, reluctantly, I stood. I was humbled before God, before man and before myself.

I was the first one at the front but people flowed in like a lost flock in a desert that had finally found water. They came by the hundreds. To my right was a beautiful Southern belle, crying. In front of me, kneeling, was a white-haired couple expensively dressed. To the left was a roughened oil-rig worker with grime under his fingernails. Next to him loomed a teenage basketball star who wore his school jacket covered with varsity letters and awards. Everyone at the front of this stage, now an altar, seemed to be near God.

I was realistic and sober when James Robison asked us to repeat a prayer with him. I heard myself saying, "Lord Jesus, I want the gift of eternal life. I am a sinner and have been trusting myself. Right now I renounce my confidence in myself and put my trust in Thee. I accept you as my personal Savior. I believe you died for my sins and I want you to come into my life and save me. I want you to be the Lord and Master of my life. Help me to turn from my way and follow you. I am not worthy, but I thank you, Lord, for saving me. Amen."

We all finished our request to God and my next sensation was beyond the words of the world. A vibration shot from the top of my head to the bottom of my feet, like a current of pure truth pushing out the old Peter and putting in a new me. It still seemed too simple. But I felt clearer, cleaner and different from ever before in my life. Something transforming had happened to me here.

I felt a smile on my face and the glow of heaven

around me. My soul had been like a wavering compass needle, but now it finally pointed to true north. I had found my lifetime direction. The salty breezes stroked me and I realized God was like the wind. I could feel Him everywhere.

Now I knew what people meant when they sang "Amazing Grace."*Even though deciding to be a Christian was a big step toward God, it was still *only* that first step. I remember thinking at the time, *Peter, how could you have waited so long to get HERE!* Today, I'm just thrilled that I made it. There's so much keeping people away from Him.

That step was only the beginning of a road to heaven I will be traveling as long as I'm on earth. I'm thrilled about getting there, but I plan to enjoy the journey as much as I can.

The night I "got saved," Mary said that the angels in heaven sang, just for me. Well, when I get to heaven, I plan to sing those angels a song of celebration they'll never forget!

I have no greater joy than to hear that my children walk in truth.

3 John 4

4

The Wedding

The piano music soothed my nerves as I stood peeking through the double doors, waiting to walk down the aisle and become Mrs. Peter Jenkins. There were about two hundred people sitting in the auditorium—M.C. and Miss Margaret from Orville, Alabama, the Walkers from Birmingham, John and Charlotte Stack from Mississippi, my girlfriends from campus, Ann, Sandy, Peggy, Beth, Emily, and many more. Peter's family was here after riding a Greyhound bus all the way from Connecticut to New Orleans. My parents had driven their camper down from Missouri. Jan and Bob Taggart were here from Moss Point; so were Bill and Jandy Hanks, and many of Peter's friends including Alvaro from Greenwich.

Today was a sunny Saturday afternoon in New Orleans, almost springlike for this seventh day of February. My mother had very little to say to me in the dressing room before the service started, but she did say, "Happy is the bride the sun shines on."

All the familiar faces turned toward me as the wedding march, "Faith of Our Fathers," began. We had chosen this old hymn for the march instead of the traditional wedding processional.

Welch Hill, one of Peter's buddies from the Baptist Seminary, was an usher and doorkeeper. In very proper fashion, I held my head erect and began the long walk toward Reverend Green and Peter, who were waiting for me at the platform. Everyone stood. I felt honored, but also more frightened than ever before in my life. Just walking down this aisle and getting married was frightening enough, but walking the rest of the way across America with Peter was quite another matter. It still troubled me.

My long white dress with a cape and hood made me look like I was from biblical times instead of the modern bride with a veil over her face. I had not been able to afford a fancy gown but had found this dress on sale at J. C. Penney. It was a simple dress but elegantly trimmed with a line of pearls down the front and around the sleeves and hood.

The walk down the aisle took only a minute or two, but within that time every obstacle Peter and I had overcome, all the work planning this day, all the unusual things that had happened during our eight-month courtship flashed through my mind. None of the people gazing at me had any idea how hard the decision had been to marry Peter. Nor had it been easy to have a wedding with almost no money. Peter had been writing his article for *National Geographic*, hoping it would someday be accepted, but he would not be paid until the story was published. I earned about a hundred dollars a month working part-time as a secretary for one of the professors and had a few dollars in savings left from my job as a social worker. Our total resources amounted to a few hundred dollars.

We had decided not to ask either of our parents to help finance our wedding because we had both been on our own for several years and how could we make them understand our unusual plans? Most people thought we were nuts, anyway, so Peter and I decided we would take care of our own wedding, regardless of how unconventional or poor it was, and have a good time anyway.

Fresh flowers had been out of the question, so we found a little shop to make a bridal bouquet, some corsages, and boutonnieres out of silk flowers. The bill came to one hundred dollars. We really had to count our pennies now. Instead of decorating the church with candelabra, flowers, and ribbons, we had decided to rent some palm trees and put them on the stage behind the preacher. Unfortunately, the trees had not been delivered on time. All the guests had arrived, everything else was in place, but the palm trees were still nowhere in sight. Peter greeted each guest at the front door, telling how excited he was to be getting married and that he was waiting on some trees! The piano music began on schedule, then went on and on and on for almost thirty minutes until the palms were delivered at the front door. Peter lifted the heavy clay pots, each holding one skinny tree, and hurriedly walked them down the aisle, placing the trees in a semicircle on the platform.

As I walked slowly toward my future husband, the palms looked like little green sprouts growing on the stage.

And then there had been the decision about our wedding cake. We had priced one at a bakery but it was too much, costing fifty-four dollars for the smallest size. So, we made it ourselves. We bought ten yellow cake mixes, and one large piece of plywood and went to work. A black woman named Izella, who worked at the women's dorm, helped. She showed us how to add lots of margarine for better taste. The cakes were baked in flat pans and then laid side by side on the plywood to make a giant sheet cake. Peter and I finished off the cake by icing it with thick, white frosting and bordering the edge with fresh pine branches. We set a little thirty-five-cent plastic bride and groom on top.

Many other necessary wedding traditions—a rehearsal dinner, a band for the reception, and even a honeymoon—had been cut due to our budget. Our blood tests and physical exams had been donated by Dr. John Potter, a physician in the congregation at Word of Faith Temple. The wedding invitations had been written and designed by Peter and me. We drew a picture of Jesus at the top of the paper and then a map of the United States below. We marked a dotted line for our proposed route across the country and invited each person on our list to come share in our joy. Part of the writing on the invitation sounded like a high school poem: "You will find friends, farmers, faculty, families, food, financiers, fun, fishermen, fathers, and faith at the reception following in the church."

And the reception would be without hors d'oeuvres, elegant china, and champagne. Instead, the women of the church donated punch and finger sandwiches to be served on paper plates we bought at Walgreen's. No stunning centerpieces would adorn the tables, just simple candles on paper doilies sitting on tablecloths rented for a total of $4.66 from an industrial laundry. Extra paper doilies had been hung on the walls to make the reception room, the church gymnasium, fit the occasion.

A few more steps and I would be on stage. My eye caught our special friend, Wally Hebert, who had sung a moving song just before the wedding march. He had accompanied himself with his guitar, and his mellow voice had made him sound like a troubadour as he sang, "If love does not flow through me, then I am nothing, Jesus reduce me to love." Peter had joined one of Wally's songs by playing a high-pitched recorder. Another friend of mine, Jan Taggart, had sung "To God Be the Glory," and Bill Hanks, a Baptist preacher, had given a moving talk about God's love and our love for each other. I had seen and heard everything from behind the double doors where I waited to walk down the aisle.

And what about our rings? My mind clamored. Did the maid of honor, Charlotte Stack, have Peter's ring? What would we do about my ring? Just seconds before I had entered the double doors to walk down the aisle, Peter's twenty-year-old brother, Freddy, almost had made my heart stop. He was Peter's best man and was supposed to hand Peter the ring to put on my finger. Our wedding rings were not single bands of gold, but were "puzzle rings" that could be taken apart and reassembled with secret directions. Since we had not figured out the intricate instructions about how to get them back together, we had tied a small string around each ring so that no one would accidentally pull them apart. Just before making my grand entrance, Freddy had held up my wedding ring, completely apart, dangling the pieces from side to side with a mischievous grin on his face.

All of this danced through my head as I took one stride and then another. I was almost to the end of the aisle. I was almost married. I was almost standing beside my sweetheart, who was dressed in a second-hand sport coat with a new shirt and tie he had found, both coming to a total of twenty dollars.

Reverend Charles Green, pastor of Word of Faith, opened his Bible. We stood with our backs to the audience ready to repeat our vows. This was a big moment.

"As I read from the inspired Word of God, your responses to each other and to God will be an eternal covenant," Reverend Green said. A solemn mood spread throughout the church. He read from the Bible: "The LORD God said, 'It is not good for the man to be alone; I will make him a helper suitable for him.' And the LORD God fashioned into a woman the rib which He had taken from the man, and brought her to the man....For this cause a man shall leave his father and his mother, and shall cleave to his wife; and they shall become one flesh."

Peter and I had selected our vows from the Bible. Peter said first, "It is not good for me to be alone so God made you. I will leave my father and mother and cleave to you as my wife and we shall become one."

I followed. "God made me a helper suitable for you. I

will be bone of your bones and flesh of your flesh. We shall become one."

Our eyes met above the script from which we were reading. Our souls were already connected.

Reverend Green read again, "Let marriage be held in honor...and the marriage bed be undefiled.... Let your character be free from the love of money, being content with what you have; for He Himself has said, 'I will never desert you, nor will I ever forsake you.' "

We both said we would hold our marriage in honor and let our character be free from the love of money.

The preacher looked at me and read: "An excellent wife, who can find?...The heart of her husband trusts in her, and he will have no lack of gain. She does him good and not evil all the days of her life."

I looked at Peter, my red-bearded young man, and with all the love I could shine through my eyes said that his heart could trust in me for "I will do you good and not evil all the days of my life."

Peter looked back at me, flashed a smile the whole world could see, and said, "I will love, nourish, and cherish you, Barbara, as Christ does the church."

We were almost through saying our vows, and I was beginning to panic about my ring. What would Peter do? What was going to happen when the pastor asked him to place the ring on my finger?

"You husbands likewise, live with your wives in an understanding way, as with a weaker vessel, since she is a woman; and grant her honor as a fellow heir of the grace of life, so that your prayers may not be hindered," Reverend Green spoke to Peter. Then to me he said, "Let not your adornment be merely external...let it be the hidden person of the heart, with the imperishable quality of a gentle and quiet spirit which is precious in the sight of God."

It was time to exchange rings. Reverend Green asked

Peter what gift he had to offer me as a sign of his love and commitment. Peter confidently turned toward Freddy. I was afraid to look and knew that the whole wedding was going to be ruined. I took a deep breath. How would the preacher handle this? Peter would probably start laughing. Freddy had that same prankster grin on his face as he handed something to Peter. The mercury lights overhead caught a sparkle.

Peter reached down and lifted my left hand. He tenderly eased a set of diamonds, big as marbles, onto my ring finger. Immediately, I recognized the rings; they belonged to Charlotte, my maid of honor, one of my long-time friends. I glanced over and she was smiling, reassuring me that everything was all right and that she had come to the rescue. No one in the audience knew that I was about to be married with someone else's ring!

"With this ring," Peter started to chuckle, then caught himself, "I give you, Barbara, my mind, spirit, and body— my total self as Christ gave Himself for the Church."

Then I took the ring for Peter and said, "With this ring, I give you, Peter, my spirit, mind, and body—my total self in obedience to our Lord's command."

Reverend Green said, "You may kiss the bride, if you wish."

"I wish," Peter said.

The congregation stood while Peter and I knelt. Peter prayed into the microphone so everyone could hear: "Lord Jesus, I dedicate our marriage to the service of God through Jesus Christ, and I hope we all can have a good time at the reception."

Reverend Green turned us around to face the people and put his hands on our heads for his final blessing: "We pray that the God who has brought Peter and Barbara together in such strange circumstances shall cause them to keep in their heart who they must serve and whose they are. We ask that God strengthen them so that in their hour of need or time of trouble, that 'one will chase a thousand but two will put ten thousand to flight.' These blessings we ask upon them in the name of Jesus our Lord."

We locked arms and marched out, husband and wife, through the smiling faces, ready to conquer the world.

5

No Turning Back

Dogs barked all night long and kept me awake. The sleeping arrangements weren't the most comfortable anyway—a sleeping bag on the ground. This was some kind of adventure. I was tired and ached all over. My hip bones felt like they had been scraped with sandpaper for a week, rubbed raw from the padded belt on my backpack. My shoulders and back hurt, too. It wasn't easy carrying thirty pounds and walking ten to twenty miles a day. We were finally on the road, headed west out of New Orleans, across Louisiana, through swamp country in one-hundred-degree weather. It was July, 1976.

This tropical climate was so muggy, I felt like I was under water. Each step required effort, like pushing against an invisible wall. We were walking the only acceptable route across southern Louisiana, Highway 90. We purposely avoided interstates in order to see more back country, but seeing anything was hard through the stream of sweat that dripped off my brow and into my eyes.

This was our fourth week on the road. I had thought

49

all along that once we got started, I would stop questioning whether I was supposed to be doing this. I had hoped that all the secret, nagging doubts would vanish and I would be overwhelmed by the excitement and adventure of walking across America. *God miraculously called me to do this,* I kept telling myself.

"Isn't this fantastic!" Peter yelled back at me. "To have your entire house on your back. No lawns to cut, no bills to pay, no babies crying. Unbelievable! Isn't it incredible, to be out of the rush and rat race? Barbara? Isn't it great?"

"Yeah. Great," I mumbled. My head was lowered as I wiped another rag full of sweat off my face.

My feet were covered with open blisters and looked like fresh-ground hamburger. I had bandaged them a few days before with gauze, but they still bled and hurt. I hobbled along, at least five block lengths behind Peter, limping with every step, wiping away a few tears along with the sweat.

Peter stopped and turned toward me, waiting. He didn't like getting too far ahead or out of hollering distance. He was annoyed with me for lagging so far behind. His face was grim.

"You should win an academy award for acting like a ninety-year-old woman," he said with a smirk. He turned and marched ahead.

I purposely dragged along, seething inside. Besides enduring the pain, I already had walked six smothering miles without a drop of water or a bite of food. I felt dehydrated, humiliated by Peter's comment, and ready to fight. It didn't help that almost every passing car would slow down to a crawl so the people inside could stare at us. Our canteens had been empty since the night before because we had not found a place to fill them. There were no fresh streams or springs to get water, only gas stations, stores, or cafés. We were deep into swamp country, rice fields, and sugar cane farms. I wanted either a drink of water or a fist fight. Nothing in between would do.

We were inching toward a small community called Iowa, Louisiana. Walking at two miles an hour, we were still more than thirty minutes from town but a house was not too far ahead. Through my dripping sweat, I could see someone walking to the road from that farm house. The person looked like an older woman. Yes, it was an elderly woman going out to her mailbox. She looked like my own grandmother. I thought, *bet she's sweet, too*, through a half grin.

I would hurry and reach her before she went back into the house. I would ask her for a cup of water. Just water, that's all I wanted. My throat was so dry it hurt to swallow. She would understand and gladly help out.

I stepped up my pace. I could see her place more clearly. A statue of Christ stood in the front yard, and another of Mother Mary overlooked a flower garden. Great! This woman was a Christian. Not only was she the grandmother type, she loved the Lord, too.

I began to wave at her, lifting my empty canteen in the air, moving it back and forth so she would get the message from a distance. Surely, she would understand. All I wanted was water. And, she could tell I was a woman, probably like her own granddaughter. I walked faster and started shouting, "Hello...Hello...Hello...Hello, ma'am..." My mouth and throat cracked. I had sweated every drop of moisture from my body, and yelling with such a dry throat hurt.

She saw me! Thank God. *Now, I will get some water and I'll have the strength to make an issue out of Peter's calling me a ninety-year-old woman. Just wait.* The old woman took a long look at me, waving my canteen and shouting. I just knew she was about to head for the hydrant and hose in her front yard. I could see them from here, next to the statue of Christ. She probably watered her flowers every evening with Mother Mary and Christ guarding over the beautiful blossoms.

The little old woman walked down her driveway, up the steps, and slammed her front door so hard I could hear it lock all the way from the road.

I almost dropped to the ground and cried. This was torture. *No water.* I was not going to get a drink of water. How could she do that—with Christ in the front yard? Couldn't she tell that I was a safe person? I felt like I was in shock, about to die, and she had pulled the plug on me. Anger, as hot as the Louisiana sun beating down, swelled in me. This was one of the most unfair, unjust, un-Christlike, mean things I had ever experienced. Just a cup of cold water was all I wanted. I would have begged for it.

I walked on in disbelief. I asked God to punish her with His wrath. Sweat poured off my forehead as I trudged ahead.

With each step my steamy anger started to evaporate. It occurred to me why the old woman must have been frightened. How many times in her life had she seen someone backpacking across Louisiana? Down her road? In front of her house? Waving something in the air and shouting at her? How could she tell I was a woman? Certainly not by the way I was dressed.

I had forgotten that people couldn't tell, very easily, if I was male or female because I carefully disguised myself. My long curly hair was up in a hat, and I wore long bermuda shorts, heavy combat boots, sunglasses, and usually a man's shirt. Only a close observer could tell that I was a woman. What my clothes didn't cover, my backpack did.

Poor old woman. She must have thought I was from Mars or maybe was another Charles Manson type. People expect to see hikers in Colorado in the high mountains, but not in the swamps of Louisiana in the middle of summer. Nothing moves in this heat, except mosquitoes and snakes. Even they use a little discretion and wait until after high noon. It was too hot to talk, to fight, to do anything except keep plodding ahead, hoping to get to water.

More than half an hour later, we entered the outskirts of Iowa, and the first building we came to was a bar. Cars were already parked out front. I supposed that people started drinking around here early in the day to escape the awful heat. There were no windows in the building, only a solid front door. What would my seminary friends think now? I would have done almost anything for water and going into this dingy bar was one of them.

We took off our backpacks and carried them inside. Since there were no windows, we were afraid that if left outside someone might steal the packs. Three men sat at the bar, hunched over, leaning on their elbows looking down into their mugs of beer. They all turned their heads slowly toward us but were either too drunk to act alarmed or had learned from past experience not to ask questions in a bar.

A country song wailed loudly from the juke box, the female singer saying something about her man running around on her and she'd be sleeping alone again tonight. There seemed to be an unspoken code here. No one talked. The barmaid came over and said, "What ya gonna have?"

All we wanted was water, but from the tone of her voice, we knew we had better order something. "Two Cokes, please, with lots of ice," Peter answered.

She slammed down two bottled Cokes and two tall bourbon glasses with a couple of ice cubes in each. A cigarette hung out from the corner of her mouth. One of her eyes was half closed, to keep the trails of smoke from burning her eyes, and she talked out of the side of her mouth.

"Two dollars," she barked.

Cokes are expensive in here, I thought. But the fizzy liquid tasted as good as pure spring water and we both had another round. We didn't dare ask the barmaid for water. She acted like we were hippies or useless trash and she wasn't about to give us the time of day. The sooner we paid for our Cokes and got out of her bar, the better off things would be.

After cooling off in the air conditioning and reviving with the cold Cokes, we were ready to leave the dark, smoky bar. We stood and helped each other with our backpacks. Peter always lifted my pack while I stepped backwards into it;

then I would buckle up and tighten all the straps. In a way, it was like saddling a horse and sometimes I felt like one, carrying all that weight. When we would gear up, people always watched, spellbound, unable to hide their curiosity, and the woman and the customers in this bar stared at us in a hard-hearted way.

"Sure would be nice *not* to have to work fer a livin'," a coarse voice said as we walked out the barroom door, back into the glaring, bright sun.

The highway was busy with traffic going toward town. Every car that passed slowed, the people inside craning their necks to get an eyeful. Although we had been on the road almost a month, I was still not used to pointing fingers and honking car horns. We were a real novelty. People looked as if they were either amazed or horrified.

Why am I doing this? I asked myself. *Am I a martyr or what? Who in his right mind would put himself through this voluntarily?* It had been seven days since I'd had a bath, and I couldn't stand how I smelled. Another night with Peter in that dirty tent? He smelled dirty, too. His breath was enough to singe the hair on my legs, which were like a briar patch because I hadn't shaved them in so long.

We had finally made it to the center of town and were looking for a café where we could buy a meal. We halted at a stoplight and were waiting for it to turn green when a carload of middle-aged women stopped for the red light. They all looked at us, especially me, in disbelief. They could tell I was a woman. They were obviously on their way to a luncheon, fashion show, or club meeting of some kind, with their fresh hairdos, bright red fingernails, tailored suits, and layers of makeup. They looked so proper and perfect, sitting in the big air-conditioned car. Not a hair out of place, no hint of sweat, no sign of any kind that any of them had been outside that day, or that week, or maybe ever.

I was about to cross the street in front of them. Their

faces were like chiseled stone, expressionless. They would never have guessed that I had been a social worker, that I had just left a Baptist seminary where I was working on a master's degree in religious education, that I had boxes of pretty clothes packed away, that I had been a beauty queen in college, that I was an A student while in school, that I was....

The light turned, and I stepped forward, down off the sidewalk and toward their car. Instantly, simultaneously, I heard four loud clicks. Every door on the car was immediately locked. The women kept watching, never taking their eyes off me. Couldn't they see what a fine person I was? Why were they afraid? When I looked down to watch my step, I realized how I must look wearing heavy combat boots and dirty socks, covered in sweat, my hair matted and stringy, my clothes wrinkled, no makeup. I was sure the Vaseline I had smeared on my face that morning to help hold in the moisture and keep my skin from chafing did not impress them. I probably looked like a combat hippie ready to attack. I felt their fear.

I wanted to stop in the middle of the intersection and scream, to force them to stop thinking we were bums or criminals. Why did everybody misunderstand? I felt helpless, not able to defend myself or explain. If only they could see past our appearance and into our hearts. I took a deep breath, held my head straight and high, ignored their wary eyes, and walked across the street. I used my best stride, the one I had learned in modeling classes. The women in their cool car never took their eyes off us.

For our light affliction, which is but for a moment, is working for us a far more exceeding and eternal weight of glory.

2 Corinthians 4:17

6

The Alligator Camp

The landscape was beginning to turn from stagnant pools of brackish water and swamps to open farm land, pastures full of cattle, horses, and soybean fields. The temperature still soared but we would be stopping soon in Westlake with Preacher and Bobbie Hebert.

We arrived at the Hebert's home in mid-August, although it felt like Christmas to me to be off the road awhile, sleeping in a bed, with air conditioning and without horns honking and people staring. The Heberts were the parents of our special friend, Wally, who had sung in our wedding and was a student at the seminary where Wally and I had attended some classes together. Wally had told us that if we walked through Westlake, his folks would be glad for us to stay with them awhile.

"There's always something going on at home," Wally had said. "We had a house full of people when I was growing up—grandparents, aunts, and uncles living with us; your visit won't be anything out of the ordinary."

Preacher was sixty-nine and had been retired for three

57

years. He was a shy, quiet man with a constant grin on his face. He stood tall, and his black eyes and hair made it clear he was from Cajun descent. His skin had a perpetual brownness, like a year-round tan. His hands were great in size.

Preacher had been a professional baseball player in his youth, with the Browns from St. Louis in the 1930s. They called him "Preacher" back then because he wasn't loud, aggressive, or out to make himself into a star. He was kind and went about his business, so the other players nicknamed him "Preacher." Being quiet did not keep him from striking out Babe Ruth and becoming famous in his own right.

Preacher's wife made up for his quietness with a magnetic personality. Nannie Locke Bostick, better known as Bobbie, was full of sparkle. Now in her sixties she had borne two girls and three boys, with Wally being the first-born son. Although all her children were grown and had families of their own, Bobbie was still in the middle of everything. She loved the bustle of her grandchildren in the yard and the banging of the door when they came in and out. The more people around, the happier she was.

"My main concern in life is for my children; I just want them to be happy," she said. "I'm just a run-of-the-mill grandmother who never wants my grandchildren to get fussed at or punished."

We became like a part of their big family, eating lots of rice and the fresh shrimp Preacher brought home. Since he had retired, he spent most of his time fishing, shrimping, and once a year, trapping alligators. He was known as the best alligator skinner in the country. While Preacher was out in his boat, Bobbie stayed home and kept up with all the family. And she kept up with her soap operas, her favorite being "The Young and the Restless."

She giggled like a schoolgirl. "Preacher does his thing and I do mine and we get along just great."

We were here at the perfect time. It happened only

once a year, only in Louisiana, and it would be a great adventure. It was alligator season. Peter was ecstatic. He wanted to go with Preacher to the swamp to trap, so we decided to stay longer. Another challenge. Another adventure for Peter. Women were not allowed to trap with the men, so I was meant to stay at home.

The day before the men were to leave for the swamp, Peter and I, while taking an afternoon stroll alone, had the bad blow-up that had been brewing for some time. In my opinion the walk across America was not working out. I was discouraged and angry. We had only been married six months and most of that time we had been training for the walk. Peter had worked on the oil rig, and the last six weeks we had been on the road. What kind of way was that to start a marriage?

Most of the time I was so exhausted, sweaty, and dirty that I didn't want to be close to Peter. We both looked and smelled terrible. Then, when we were rested, clean, and together, we were in someone else's home. There was no time to be alone and to nurture our relationship except on the road under severe physical stress. I was a newlywed with blisters on my feet, burned skin, and a husband who was more excited about alligators than me.

The more I told Peter how I felt, the angrier I became. I exploded. Hysteria seemed calm compared to the condition I was in. I tried to explain what I was going through. Why wasn't I having fun like Peter? Why was this walk so hard for me? Why wasn't Peter more compassionate? Why wasn't our marriage more normal? Why did everything about us have to be so radical?

The more I said, the more Peter purposely avoided the subject, staring at the trees, whistling for a dog out of someone's yard. This made me crazy with anger. I thought all of this was terribly unfair. After all, Peter had already walked from New York to New Orleans, had been on the road more than a year and a half, and was an experienced hiker. I had never been camping in my life and had never walked more than a mile, much less with thirty pounds on my back.

"Cool it! You're ruining the whole thing," Peter finally snapped. "If you'd stop being so rebellious, maybe you could get your act together. You try to put all the blame on me; but if you want to blame somebody, then blame God!"

"You can take this walk and shove it! I'm sick of you, sick of blisters and sore muscles, tired of your callous attitude toward me, sick of..." I shouted in tears. My voice cracked with fury. "You're the biggest jerk I've ever known."

"Why don't you grow up and act like a mature adult!" Peter countered. "You think you're the only one who ever had a problem. Why don't you quit feeling sorry for yourself. And stop whimpering. Sometimes I wish I could cry, too," he said, mocking my tears.

At dawn the next day we were on our way by boat to the alligator camp. The camp was six miles back into the swamp and the only way in or out was by boat. Somehow, Preacher had found a way for me to go along and trap gators with the men. I was glad but still smoldering over the argument with Peter. I was so cross about our fight that I was pondering how I could quit the walk. Enough was enough! Surely we would be better off if I went back to the seminary, finished my degree, and met Peter at the end of the walk. I could drive out to meet him on the road a few times. My plan had been brewing in my mind all night, and I was going to break the news to him while we were at the alligator camp. Even if Peter was insensitive, I didn't want our fight to keep me from having an adventure, too.

I spoke to Peter only when he would speak to me. As far as I was concerned, our fight was still pending, with storm clouds hanging in the air. He was so pumped up with excitement, our argument appeared to be history to him now. He smiled into the morning sun as we sped down the canals, gliding through the swamps and rushes. Other men would be there; this was really big stuff.

Peter asked Preacher one question after another, probing him like a detective for every piece of information about alligators. The setting was wild and beautiful. Brilliant yellow and white lillies bloomed on the banks and every now and then we heard a splash of water.

"Another gator," Preacher would say. We jumped each time and twisted our heads hoping to see it. "These waters are full of 'em."

With the rising sun, my heart rose a little, too. I watched Peter out of the corner of my eye, and the electricity in his face made me want to forget what had happened the day before. His eyes were filled with wanderlust. His ruddy complexion was aglow in the early morning light, and I couldn't help falling in love with him all over again. I wanted to hang onto my wounded pride, but the ice inside me was beginning to melt. His carrot-red beard, blond hair, crystal blue eyes, and headstrong ways made me wonder if he had Viking blood in his veins. *If only he would be more aware of me as a woman, different from himself, and treat me with more tenderness,* I thought. Our boat slowed and thumped against the dock. It was time to unload our gear at the camp. *Maybe we'll get our relationship worked out one of these days,* I decided as I grabbed my duffle bag. I guessed that was why God meant for marriage to last a lifetime; it must take a lot of life to make a marriage work.

A houseful of people were waiting—Preacher's brother-in-law, Stoner; Glen Hebert, a distant relative; Mrs. Charles Hebert, the cook and owner of the camp; and an older couple named Moore visiting from Oklahoma. There were others, their names I couldn't remember at first meeting. We were shown to our bunkroom and told how things would be done while we were there.

Glen explained how we would go into the marshland in a mud boat, a special craft with a souped-up Chevrolet engine that could speed through shallow water and mud. We would bait a long rope with a dead blackbird. When the rope was under water, we would know there was a gator on the other end. Two or three men would pull the fighting gator out of the water, and then Glen would use a .22 caliber pistol or 30-30 rifle to shoot the gator in the head, after which the gator would be tagged and brought in for skinning. Today, we were going out to check the twenty-six traps. Glen said that they had permits to get 114 alligators this year.

"Some people's got it, and some ain't," Glen said. "But Preacher here is one of the best. He can skin an eight-foot gator in one hour."

The mud boat had been off limits for women. I was the first female allowed to go with the men to get the gators. Before I could absorb all that Glen had told us, we were headed through the sixteen thousand acres of marshland. Glen yelled over the loud engine that the female gator had to be six years old to lay eggs, usually forty at a time, and she would lay them in straw beds in the sunshine. He pointed to spots where he knew there were nests. A mother gator was dangerous and would attack if her little ones were in danger. Preacher hollered that we would try to catch male gators and they had to be at least four feet long.

"Them male gators beller just like a bull," Preacher said. The grin on his face broadened. I could tell he was excited. There was an untamed, prehistoric mood in everyone. I felt as if we were going into a time and place unknown to modern civilization.

"Contact!" Glen shouted. That meant full speed ahead. Tunnels of black thick mud sprayed out the back of the boat. The engine was as loud as a freight train and felt as powerful. I wore a headscarf to keep my hair from blowing and to wipe mud off my face. We slid through a narrow trail of high grass and saw that the blackbird was gone. The rope was submerged, like a fishing line, alongside the bank. Glen stopped the motor.

"Looks good," Glen said.

"Bet it's a big one," Preacher said as he, Glen, and Peter began pulling on the rope. The rope tightened. Then it began to swing back and forth, and shortly, there was a loud slap of water.

"Watch the tail!" Glen yelled. "He can knock us out of the boat. Got to get him up, get his head out of the water."

My heart was in my throat and beating as loud as a drum. The men were all fighting with the rope trying to hang on. The gator was a big one. Everyone was yelling.

"Watch out!"

"Pull!"

"Easy now."

"Don't let go!"

"Slack up a little."

The gator was hooked good. He had swallowed the blackbird, and the giant hook was lodged in his stomach. He couldn't get loose, unless the men lost the rope.

"Man, he's one of the biggest ones I've seen in a long time," Preacher said in short breaths.

The massive tail arched out of the black water and slammed down with a wallop that would have killed a man. The gator lifted his head, opened his foot-long mouth and growled.

"He's at least a four-hundred pounder!" Glen shouted.

"Around fifty years old, too," Preacher gasped.

Our boat rocked from side to side as the men fought with the rope. Peter, Glen, and Preacher were all standing, trying to keep their balance. Peter accidentally stepped too far to one side.

"Don't move or you'll turn us over!" Glen yelled at Peter. "Just hang onto the rope and stand still."

"What'll happen if we turn over?" Peter asked.

"Nobody will be around to tell," Preacher said.

Glen pulled the pistol from the holster on his waist. Peter and Preacher braced themselves and gave one final yank on the rope. The knotty head slapped from side to side.

"Close your mouth!" Glen screamed at the gator as he aimed the pistol at his head. He had to shoot him right between the eyes to kill him and Glen couldn't do that with the gator's mouth open.

The gator's teeth looked like they were two inches long. He growled, twisted, banged his tail against the boat, splashed up and down, and in one instant, raised his head as he sped toward the boat.

Boom...Boom...Blood spewed everywhere. More splashing. The fifty-year-old gator was dead.

Back at camp everyone marvelled over the gator, which measured ten feet long. He was a once-in-a-lifetime catch, and Peter and I had been part of the excitement and had even helped. The story was told and retold—how we found him, how Peter had almost tipped the boat, how the gator had fought, how Glen had pulled the trigger. On and on the storytelling went until long after supper.

Most of the men were outside under an open pavilion where Preacher had started to skin the historic catch. Peter and I were inside the cabin. We could hear all the talk outside through the open window. Just as we were about to sit back on the sofa and try to solve some of our personal conflicts, the Moores came in.

They sat down in chairs next to us, and we began to chat. They were retired, living on a fixed and small income, and looked like kind-hearted people. They travelled in a camper and had been invited by the owner of the camp to come and see what trapping gators was all about. They were having a great time. "We have to leave in about a half hour," Mr. Moore said. "We've got an appointment to keep. I think Glen is going to run us back into town."

This was a polite interlude, although I was eager to have Peter to myself so we could talk. The excitement of the day had not washed away my tangled emotions. Secretly, I hoped the Moores would leave soon. I didn't know them and they didn't know us, so I was shocked by what came next. They were about to leave, and I expected just to say goodbye and "nice meeting you."

"I hope you young folks won't take offense, but I'd like to pray for you," Mr. Moore said.

Peter and I were both taken off guard. Mr. Moore quickly explained that he was a retired preacher and now travelled around the country, preaching wherever he was asked and needed. Peter and I were a little nervous, but after our fight we both knew we could use prayer.

"Why don't we kneel?" Mr. Moore asked boldly, now taking charge.

We all knelt down on the linoleum floor, right in front of the open window. I could still hear the men laughing and talking outside, over where Preacher was skinning. I hoped that no one out there would hear what was going on in here.

Mr. Moore placed a hand on each of our heads and began to pray. His voice raised, he was almost cheering he got so loud.

"The Word of The Lord has come to me today to tell you that God has truly joined you together, even before you were conceived in the womb, before you were born. You will be known from coast to coast, and from mainland to mainland. You will teach the educated, the intelligent, the poor, the humble."

I was having flashbacks to the church in New Orleans, of that fateful sermon. I trembled. I tried to hold my breath to keep my heart from pounding so loud. *How does this stranger know so much about us?* The prayer continued to tumble from Mr. Moore's lips.

"Peter, you will be a prophet and, Barbara, you have the spirit of a Lamb...Do not despair. Be patient, for God is going to teach you many things. You haven't seen anything yet...You have the gift of discerning spirits..." The loud prayer ended with a deep sigh and a soulful "Amen."

Peter and I came up from the floor like cripples, our

knees shaking. We were blown away. No one, absolutely no one knew what Peter and I were going through. No one knew anything about us except that we were walking across America. The *National Geographic* article was still a dream, and no one had ever heard of us. Preacher could not have told the Moores anything about us, because we had never talked about the Lord or religious matters with him. I was stunned. I staggered like a drunk.

Mr. Moore smiled at us through teary eyes and said he wanted to give us something. He handed us an envelope and told us not to open it until he and his wife were gone. Before we could regain our composure, the two of them had said goodbye and were propelling in the motor boat through the swamp and out of sight.

Our meeting had been happenstance. I didn't know what to think or how to act. We were solemn and reverent as we opened the envelope. What more could this couple do to shock us? Why did they choose to give us something sealed in an envelope?

Inside, folded neatly, were three worn bills. Ten dollar bills. They had probably been tucked away for safekeeping in case of an emergency. This was hard-earned money and there was no way to say thank you. The Moores were gone.

A word fitly spoken is like...an ornament of fine gold.
Proverbs 25:11–12

7

Stranger Danger

T hree months after leaving New Orleans we reached the Sabine River, which divides Louisiana from Texas. We were thrilled. This was the first running, clear water we had come across since leaving New Orleans. We swam, washed our clothes, floated like walruses, and camped in the middle of the river on a little island. The next morning after breaking camp, the second we crossed the river into east Texas, we noticed the change. Behind us were the swamps, seashells, sugar cane fields, seafood, mosquitoes, and French Catholics. Ahead lay rolling hills, fire ants, grass burrs, and cowboy hats.

We stopped at the first cafe'we came to, and the coffee tasted like the Sabine River. No longer was it thick, black, and full of chicory like the liquid mud they served in Louisiana. This stuff tasted more like brown water, but the eggs, biscuits, and gravy hit the spot. The cafe'was crowded with men, most of them truck drivers who spoke in clipped sentences. They wore jeans and boots, and their large cowboy hats rested neatly on the table tops beside them. Some laughed, some smoked, but everybody listened to the juke box which was playing tunes by Dolly Parton. A few off-color jokes were told about her. One man looked at us and spoke.

"Where ya headed?" he asked.

"West. Maybe up through Colorado," Peter answered.

"Colorado? This time of year?" He was obviously alarmed.

"Yeah. What's wrong with that?"

The man was middle-aged, robust, and looked like he chewed nails for fun. There was a crusty way about him. He shook his head in disbelief.

"Don't you know you'll freeze to death? I've been there hunting and, good Lord, it gets cold! Snow gets knee deep. Yer not very old are you?" he asked looking at me. "I'd be worried sick if my baby was out on the road like you."

Peter ignored his comments, kept on eating his break-fast, and mumbled "redneck" under his breath.

What the gruff truck driver didn't know was that I had not told my parents. If Mother and Daddy had known I was walking across America they would have been worried sick, too.

It had all been too much—our unusual courtship, the anxiety I had been through trying to decide whether or not to marry Peter, Mom Beall's sermon about "Will You Go with This Man?" Everything that had happened to me was so overwhelming that I couldn't explain it to my parents or any-one and make it sound sane. I had enough turmoil in my own heart without knowing my parents were upset, too. So I had decided to wait and tell them after I had proven I could tackle this challenge. I would let them know what I was doing when we reached Dallas. All they knew was that Peter and I were traveling around the country, collecting material for an ar-ticle in *National Geographic* magazine. I didn't lie. I simply didn't tell them our "traveling" was on foot.

This was the most beautiful day of our entire trip. The sky was clear and the air so crisp it made me light-headed. I had never felt so invigorated, so peaceful, and so free. The troubling thoughts of the past months had ebbed and it seemed that the cooler air, the fall leaves, and the rolling hills were helping me think more clearly than at any time since we had left steamy New Orleans. The miles of sweat and tears, the prayer at the alligator camp, and now the revitalizing briskness of autumn were like puzzle pieces suddenly locking together. I sensed that there really was a purpose to all I had experienced, and the veil that had covered my eyes was lifting. I was seeing beyond my blisters, aches, and combat boots.

We were getting closer to Dallas, the first major city we would come to on foot. The thought of coming to a metropolis, after nothing but small towns, cafés, and country grocery stores excited me. What might be in store for us there? I longed to sleep on a bed, although I had adjusted to sleeping on the ground.

Last night had been an exception. As always we had chosen our campsite right at dusk so that no one could spot us. We never built a fire or left evidence of our campsite. We did this because we never knew whose land we were camping on, and it would have been too time-consuming and difficult to locate an owner and ask permission. We camped in tree groves, tall cornfields, behind thick brushes, sometimes under bridges. But we always stopped just before dark so no one could find us. Then we rose early, left the land the way we found it, and were on the road before anyone knew where we had camped. We were hunting for "just the right spot" when Peter noticed the same car had passed us three times. It was an old green Chevrolet, not one of the trendy compact cars, but more like a big army tank. On the third time, he brought it to my attention. I usually watched the ground, noticed flowers and butterflies, sang, thought about life, often talked to God or to myself without watching the traffic. Peter did that. He was very vigilant and hawklike.

"Come on, we got to split!" Peter said sharply.

"What?" I asked, coming back to reality and out of my daydream.

"That car has been following us and the guy looks suspicious."

"Peter, I think you're a little too jumpy." I was feeling mellow and not in the mood to be pushed.

"Take my word for it, that guy is strange. I can feel it."

The car passed us slowly for the fourth time and rounded a curve. Without being obvious, I looked the man over. He seemed to be about thirty years old, was fair skinned, kind of balmy-looking with light hair. He did look creepy. As soon as the car was out of sight, Peter said, "Let's get outta here."

Without another word we jumped the roadside ditch, which was full of weeds—a perfect spot for snakes. We ran as fast as we could, our packs heaving and bouncing, into a forest of overgrown brush and tall pines. It was nearly dark as we entered the thicket and it seemed like we had stepped into a deep cave.

"Can't take any chances," Peter whispered as we crouched low. We were silent as rabbits. The car passed again moving very slowly with headlights on. Peter was right.

"That's the same car we passed a few miles back, stopped on the side of the road and the driver was leaning under the hood. Remember?" Peter asked.

"No, honey. I didn't pay any attention," I whispered. I realized how Peter always was on guard. It never occurred to me to watch other people along the road or to be cautious.

"What are we gonna do?" I said.

"Sh-h-h...Stay put. Don't make a move."

The car stopped right in front of the woods. The driver rolled down the window and looked into the blackness where we were hidden. We held our breath. I remembered Huckleberry Finn's hiding in the cave. At least three or four minutes passed while we hunched down, peeping through the brush.

"Never know, he could pull a gun...Shoot us," Peter whispered so low I could barely hear.

My heart jumped. Dear Lord, I had never thought of such a thing! I quickly remembered reading the newspaper headline this morning at the café, "Campers Shot in the Head." I was thankful for Peter's wariness. In the few months of our marriage I had learned that when Peter said he had a bad feeling about something, he usually had good cause. In fact, I was listening to Peter more and more and respecting his judgment. Although still an independent, headstrong career gal, I was slowly changing my opinion of Peter and his role as a man.

By now it was so dark we could barely see the man's face. Yet, even in the edge of darkness, I could see that his beady eyes had a penetrating and evil look. This was a strange and troubling moment.

"Probably on dope," Peter mumbled.

"You mean on drugs?" I asked way too loud, my voice cracking.

"Shut up...Sh-h-h-h." I could feel the scowl in Peter's retort. He ignored me, peering like an owl through the night, afraid that the man had heard my voice.

Great. Now we had a gun-toting, psychotic, drug-addicted murderer looking for us. *He's probably the one who killed the other campers*, I thought. My mind was running wild. What if he got out of the car and came looking for us? Oh, Lord! What were we going to do? We didn't have any sort of weapon, no gun, no nothing—except for Peter's pocket knife. The peculiar stillness made me sweat. I could hear the crickets and katydids, and off in the distance people were talking, probably sitting on their front porch. Other than these scattered sounds, there was a deafening hush in which my breathing sounded as loud as a hurricane wind.

The man pulled out a flashlight and shined it into the

woods. The beam of light probed from side to side, searching...searching...shining over our heads. He must have seen us.

"Get down!" Peter pushed my head to the ground.

It was time to pray. I called on the power of the Lord, I pleaded the blood of Jesus, I rebuked Satan, I reminded God that this walk was His idea and that we needed protection. On and on I went. All my seminary classes in worship leadership and religious behavior went out the door. All I knew was that I was scared and we needed help. I would push every button, say every pat formula, do whatever needed to be done to get God to step in and save us! Now I sensed the danger that Peter had felt the first time he saw the man. This man was determined to find us, and the evil force I sensed made my heart pound so hard I knew the man could hear it from the road.

We lay motionless on the ground, the minutes seemed like hours. Finally, the flashlight clicked off and we heard the motor of the car turn over. He hadn't found us. He was leaving!

Peter lifted his head an inch and peeked. The car hadn't moved. Peter's hand pressed harder on my head, again pushing my face into the bushes, making sure I didn't come up too soon. Drat! I wished Peter would let up a little. This was irritating my skin and I started to itch all over but was afraid to move.

The car idled. A couple of minutes passed. I prayed some more, hoping the man would tire of his search and give up. At last, creeping as slow as a turtle, the car moved away. I could almost feel the driver's gaze, examining every inch of the thicket, still aiming to find us. At least five more minutes ticked away before the car rounded the curve.

Peter did not sit up until long after the taillights were out of sight. "Let's not pitch the tent until we're sure he won't be back," Peter whispered.

We sat in the darkness until the moon rose to the top

of the sky. The evening stars twinkled, seeming to assure us the danger had passed. Our eyes adjusted to the darkness and we could see well enough to camp. Peter motioned. We stood up and began to unpack.

Before I could unzip the flap on my backpack, I began to itch all over. I didn't know if it was the excitement, the threat of danger or what, but I felt something crawling over my entire body. Glancing down at my light green hiking pants, I noticed little specks all over them. More of these dark spots were on my arms, and as I frantically examined myself in the moonlight, I found they were everywhere— even on my neck. Peter already had pitched the tent and was unrolling his sleeping mat inside when I shrieked.

"Peter...I'm covered with them!"

"What?" he asked, his tone of voice warning me to be more quiet.

"I'm covered with thousands of them!"

"Thousands of what?" Peter asked.

"TICKS!" I whispered hoarsely, wanting to scream.

Never had something like this happened to me. I had never seen so many ticks. Hundreds. Thousands. Maybe millions of them! The tent was already staked down, and we didn't dare to move for fear that the weird man might be parked out of sight, waiting for us to come out. There was no place to go. The ticks were crawling all over me, up my legs, under my blouse, up my neck, into my hair, everywhere.

Under the moonlight, I stripped off my clothes and shook them with a frenzy. I shuddered from both fear and the awful realization that I was covered with not two or three, but thousands of baby ticks. My mind said, "Be calm," but my nerves said, "Freak out!" As a compromise I decided all I could do was shake, twist, and jump up and down hoping to rid myself of as many of these nasty, tiny, bloodsucking things as possible. Peter had miraculously escaped and was inside the tent. The entire time we were hiding he must have lain in a spot free from the ticks while my body was buried in the middle of their favorite bush.

Like a wild cave woman, I hopped up and down under the moonlight in nothing but my underwear, looking like I was doing a rain dance or having a seizure. No one could see me except the animals of the night and they were probably stiff with curiosity, wondering if this "human" were crazy. When I stopped jumping, I heard something. It was coming from inside the tent. Peter was already snoring.

I will say of the LORD,
"He is my refuge and my fortress;
My God, in Him I will trust."
Surely He shall deliver you from the snare
   of the fowler and from the perilous pestilence.
He shall cover you with His feathers,
And under His wings you shall take refuge;
His truth shall be your shield and buckler.
You shall not be afraid of the terror by night,
Nor of the arrow that flies by day,
Nor of the pestilence that walks in darkness,
Nor of the destruction that lays waste at
   noonday.
A thousand may fall at your side,
And ten thousand at your right hand;
But it shall not come near you.

                                          Psalm 91:2–7

8

Our Last Dollar

Dallas lay straight ahead. From many miles away we could see the tips of buildings rising out of the flat prairie. Cars and trucks roared by on the highway, and we could feel the pull of the city.

Peter and I were still a day's walk away. We stopped at a gas station to get a Coke, unhooking our backpacks and sitting down on a bench to rest and absorb the warm fall sun.

The owner of the station wore overalls and had a toothpick sticking out of the corner of his mouth. The shortness of the pick showed that he had chewed on it for some time. He watched us for a long while, saying not a word. He seemed to be thinking long and hard about something. Finally, he spoke to me but pointed his finger at Peter.

"You must think an awful lot of that ugly outfit!"

"You bet," I said with a grin. Peter acted like he had not heard what the man said.

We were now deep into cattle country and oil wells were everywhere, pumping up and down like giant grasshoppers. The tall pines of Louisiana and east Texas were far behind us and the only shade available was from the mesquite, those squatty and thorny trees that withstand both the Texas sun and the tough hides of cattle rubbing against them. As we hugged the fence lines to stay off the highway, cattle followed us in single file for miles. Peter was particularly fond of the bulls and developed a "world class" bull call. He would bellow and moo-o-o and snort and the boys of the herd would follow him devotedly. The bigger the bull the better the call seemed to work. Peter appeared to feel a kinship with the bulls because of their massive size and fearless ways. Peter saw himself like that, big and bold.

Flying grasshoppers sprayed from the weeds as we walked..We had to choose our steps carefully and watch for mounds of deadly red ants in the grass. These ants were so ferocious that an army of them could take down a horse or a cow. They would bite and sting and eventually kill. And we had to watch for grass burrs, those round balls filled with sharp needles that would lodge in our socks and around our ankles.

This was a happy October day in every way except one: we had just five dollars and were entering a major city, not knowing anyone or from where our next meal would come. Our savings of eight hundred dollars had been spent walking from New Orleans to Dallas. The wind blew unhindered across a land as open and wide as the ocean. There was no place to retreat, no spot to hide and ponder our situation. We kept moving, looking toward the city in the distant haze, wondering what would happen to us. Because of our previous unusual experiences with God, we felt assured that something special would happen. Assured, but still a little worried.

Peter and I walked side by side. This was one of the good times when I could keep up with him because the air was cool and I wasn't worn out. We talked about our situation. There was no one we could call, no one we could ask to loan us money, and nowhere to stay. We knew we couldn't camp on sidewalks and parking lots in the city.

"Why don't we hold hands and pray?" I asked Peter.

With his head held high and his eyes set on Dallas, Peter said, "Lord, here we are. Please fill our stomachs, our pocketbook, and give us a place to stay. Amen."

We walked forward, the sun warming our faces. The wind was to our backs, pushing us ahead and helping to lighten our load. We were in the outskirts of Dallas, walking through Seagoville. After praying our minds into neutral, we now refused to worry about what was or was not going to happen. One step after another, we kept going.

Fifteen minutes had passed when two bicyclists headed toward us, a young man in his late twenties and a little girl. They came closer. They passed us and turned into a store parking lot. We kept walking. A few minutes later the man and child came by us again from the rear and this time they stopped.

"Hello. Where you headed?" The man asked.

"Into Dallas," Peter said.

"If you don't mind my asking, why the yellow crosses on the backpacks?"

On the back of our bright blue backpacks, we had glued iridescent yellow crosses which shined in the dark so that drivers could see us from a distance. The crosses were also our way of telling passersby that we were Christians and not to be afraid of us.

Peter gave a short, cautious reply. He was very gentle with strangers, but very shrewd, never giving out too much information too soon.

The young man was quite talkative and asked one question after another. He told us his name was Ron Hall, this was his daughter, Lisa, he lived down the road a short distance, his wife's name was Kathy, they were on their way to fix a low tire on the bicycle. How long had we been on the road? Would we like to walk to their house? Would we like to eat supper with them? He was the pastor of a small church

...Maybe we'd like to attend church with them tomorrow?

Yes, yes, indeed. A new breeze stirred the air and no one heard me whisper, "Thank you, Lord."

Ron Hall preached every Sunday at the Lighthouse Christian Center, a small frame building in the suburbs of Dallas. We arrived for worship in our best and only dress clothes. I wore a long, sheer, lightweight dress (everything I had was valued in terms of weight) that looked more like a curtain than a dress. I knew it was tacky, but the dress was cool, covered my muscular legs, and made me feel feminine again. Peter wore his only sport shirt, clean jeans, and sneakers.

About thirty people were present, most of them young families and a few old folks. Ron welcomed us, told the congregation who we were, and what we were doing. He seemed pleased to have us as visitors and proud that we were staying in his home.

"We have to trust in the Lord in everything. God works in mysterious ways, and I know he sent Peter and Barbara our way," he shouted from the top of his lungs. The old people heard him without turning up their hearing aids.

"Hallelujah! Glory to God!" someone said.

"And we've got to trust the Lord here in this church. We've got to believe He will meet our needs. We are twelve hundred dollars behind in our bills, and we've got to trust the Lord to supply."

A stillness invaded the room. No amens or hallelujahs were heard now. Just a heavy silence. Peter and I were startled and touched. Ron had taken us into his home, fed us, and given us a warm bed to sleep in without saying a word about the church's financial needs. Nor had he told us he had not drawn a salary in almost a month.

The atmosphere in this church was not like some of the bigger churches we had attended. There was no formality, no printed program. The group seemed to resemble a small circle of friends who were trying to reach God and get their problems solved.

"Would it be all right if I said something?" Peter asked as he stood up from the church pew. Ron didn't act alarmed, as though Peter were out of place.

"Please go ahead."

"I don't know what's going on here," Peter said calmly, "but I know God wants us here. Sometimes, I believe God wants us to give our all, whether it is walking across America or giving our money. And that's what He's told me to do today."

Oh, no! I thought. What is Peter going to do now? I was afraid of what was coming next. Peter explained why we were walking across America, when he had left New York, how he had become a Christian, and that he had written an article for *National Geographic.* He described many of the kinds of people we had met and then he told what God wanted him to do here, today.

"We walked into town with five dollars in our pockets and spent part of that on something to eat before your pastor came by on his bicycle and invited us home to eat with him. He gave all that he had to us, and now we want to give all that we have to you. All we have left is $1.87 to our name. And God has told me to give it to you, to this church." Peter sat down.

A heaviness seemed to hang over the people. Some lowered their heads and started to wipe away tears. Soft amens were said all across the room. Deep sighs could be heard, and someone began to sing "Amazing Grace." People locked arms, some knelt beside their pews, and some walked down and fell to their knees at the altar. One by one, members of the group started digging into their pockets, pulling out twenty-dollar bills, writing checks, and dropping handfuls of coins into the offering plates.

A knock at the door. Peter and I were resting at Ron

and Kathy's home while they were at the church. The man standing out front looked familiar, but we couldn't place the face. Where had we seen him before?

"Oh, wasn't he at the church service yesterday?" I whispered to Peter.

"Hello there, my name is Don Stevens, and I heard you speak at the church yesterday," the visitor said to Peter.

"Please come in."

"Hope I'm not interrupting anything," Don said in a timid way. He was a tall thin man, like a lanky Texas cowboy, with deep blue eyes and a shy smile. He was also very nervous, clearing his throat several times.

"Can't stay but a minute. Today is one of my free days from the fire department."

Peter and I looked at each other and wondered what this man wanted. We finally coaxed him into sitting down, but he firmly resisted drinking a cup of coffee with us.

"Oh, if it wouldn't be too much trouble, I'd like a cup," he said finally, looking up at me apologetically.

Peter was good at helping people to relax, and he began to ask this nervous man some questions. We learned that Don was close to forty years old, had been married to his wife Sarah for seven years, had a son named Douglas Glen who was four and a baby girl, Sara Lee, eighteen months old. The small talk calmed him.

"Ya know, when I heard that you'd been to a Baptist seminary," he said to me, "I knew you and my wife ought to get together. She went to a Baptist seminary, too, here in Fort Worth. She's really smart."

Don was from Muleshoe, Texas, where he had grown up and helped his dad farm. His big dream in life had not been to ride the range as a cowboy or to be a farmer, but to become a fireman. He had moved to Dallas and worked his way through the ranks while finishing college at night with honors. He was now a fire chief. Peter asked him what area of Dallas he supervised.

"All of it," Don said, blushing.

Don and Sarah were long-time Baptists but had been invited to visit the Lighthouse Christian Center, a non-denominational church. Their first visit had been yesterday.

Don shuffled his long thin legs, crossing them and un-crossing them. He looked away into the distance often, like he was trying to get up courage to say something. His hand shook when he drank his coffee, and he bowed his head frequently, as if he were about to pray. This severe shyness was something new to us, but we waited silently, not wanting to push him. Whatever he wanted to say to us seemed very hard for him.

"If it wouldn't offend y'all, Sarah and I would like to do something for you." The words came slowly, a drawl. He stopped rubbing his hands together. Whatever he was about to do, he'd never done it before.

"We've talked it over, we believe..." Don shook his head back and forth, back and forth, struggling. "We'd like to..."

He seemed unable to stand this ordeal any longer, and we didn't know how much longer we could either. Suddenly he jumped to his feet, handed Peter an envelope and blurted, "This is from the Lord."

Peter opened the envelope and pulled out fifty dollars.

"This is a lot of money," Peter said.

"I may be just a fireman, not very important, but Sarah and I know it takes a lot of courage to do what you and Barbara are doing. You'd be crazy to try something like this without real faith in God and this country of ours. I was happy to hear you tell about all the good people you've met, how we Americans tear ourselves down too much. We believe it's people like you who can help turn our land back to the Lord." The last words tumbled out, like he had practiced this speech in front of a mirror and now, relieved that he was through, he could sit down.

He didn't sit down, though, but scrambled to the front

door, waved, and said a quick goodbye.

    Yes...Yes, indeed. Thank you, Lord, again.

Give, and it will be given to you: good measure, pressed down, shaken together, and running over will be put into your bosom. For with the same measure that you use, it will be measured back to you.

Luke 6:38

9

Mysterious Ways

Peter

The fall morning air in Washington, D.C., was crisp as Barbara and I walked toward the National Geographic Society's main office, on 17th and M Streets. The date was November 3, 1976. A year had passed since I'd sent in the "article" I'd written for them about my walk from New York to New Orleans. Many times since I'd wondered what had happened to it. Would it ever be published? Finally, the two editors we had worked with, Tom Smith and Harvey Arden, had called and said that we could come to Washington because it seemed like the magazine would "probably" publish the story. Whether or not Tom Smith put more emphasis on the word *probably*, it seemed to ring much louder than any other word he said.

When my dog, Cooper, and I had first walked through Washington three years earlier, I'd stopped and talked with some of the people at *National Geographic* magazine. Before that first meeting I had pictured in my mind what the writers and photographers would look like and how they lived. The glamour of their lifestyles would make ads in the most stylish magazines seem bland in comparison, I had imagined. Every one of them would drive a chestnut-brown Porsche and live in a custom-made house on top of a hill. Their homes would be filled with exotic collectibles from all over the world, and their hair would always look like it was blowing in the wind.

In reality I had found they were all very talented, mostly low-key and thoughtful. Some of them didn't have enough hair to blow in the wind, and none of the ones I met drove a chestnut-brown Porsche. They drove station wagons, old Volvos or didn't even own cars. In real life they looked much more normal than I had imagined. Still, I was very nervous about the thought of being back in D.C. I felt so inadequate every time I read one of their excellent articles or looked at their incredible photographs. The last time I was at their office I'd said it would probably take me about five months to walk across America. The walk had already lasted three years, and I was only as far as Dallas. At best, I expected a lot of jokes about how slow I walked! I also imagined they might be bringing us here to tell us gently, "Thanks, but your photos aren't good enough and your writing is even worse. Keep walking, but we'll have to have our camera back." I was ready to give it back and keep walking.

As we waited for an editor to meet us I recalled what a confused and searching young man I'd been on that first visit. Since then my attitude about America had changed and I had become a Christian and married Barbara. Many people suggested I stop the walk in New Orleans and begin a normal life. Some people did a lot more than just suggest: they were powerfully opposed to our completing the walk. "After all," they'd say, "you've found God, a wife, and your country. What else is there?" I was thankful that they cared so much but I never thought it was quite that simple. Also, I thought of my new relationship with God as just the beginning of a long partnership.

So here I was back at *National Geographic*, a Christian. Jimmy Carter had just been elected as our President and there was much talk about this "born-again thing." I understood why so many people in America didn't know what Bible-belt Christianity meant, because I had learned that growing up in the Northeast, as I had, just "ain't the same as being born and raised in Alabama." In the South, being born-again, having revivals, going to church three times a week, and using "Lord" in your everyday conversation is commonplace, whether you're that kind of Christian or not. If you're not, you've been exposed to it. For the past three years I'd been walking and living in the South and now understood that for millions of Southerners, Christianity is not just for an hour on Sunday but a way of life.

Although faith in God had drastically changed my outlook on life, I didn't want the people I knew at *National Geographic* to think of me as some kind of religious fanatic who had the answers to everyone else's questions. My Christianity was so young, and I was still trying to figure out all that it meant to me. I wasn't ready to present it to others as *their* answer, especially people as exposed to the world and its varying views as these people. After all, they were constantly publishing stories about strange and far-off lands, detailing their different cultures, peoples, lifestyles, and religions. I knew that a lot of cultured and well-educated people, like many of these folks, thought that believing in God and trusting in Him was a bit ridiculous and an overly simplistic way of reacting to life. Whatever they believed was fine with me. I just was not ready to evangelize everyone I came into contact with.

People carrying briefcases hurried past us. Last time I'd been here I'd been dressed in sweat pants and a T-shirt. Now I wasn't dressed much better. I had on an orange and brown western shirt, corduroy pants, my walking shoes, and a sport coat I had borrowed from a friend. Barbara looked nice in a rust-colored sweater she'd bought for less than half-price and a skirt. My being an unpublished bus boy gave us very little money to spend for clothes. I was making about $145.00 a week working at a Mexican restaurant in Dallas.

A woman dressed for success in a pin-striped blue suit rushed by and dropped a manila folder full of papers. I bent down to pick them up and the scattered papers reminded me of how close we'd come to not being here.

It had all started in New Orleans, when I'd first been asked by *National Geographic* to put my thoughts down on paper. The editors said they knew that I'd never written anything before, so they gave me a month or so to see what I might say in my own words. The dean of students at the New Orleans Baptist Theological Seminary had made arrangements for me to stay in a room in one of their dorms. They felt this was wise since I was a new Christian in wild and sin-saturated New Orleans; it would be better for me there on campus. I began to write.

The problem was I had no idea what to do, where to begin, and how to keep going if I did get going. I'd never taken any writing courses in college. When I had been assigned term papers in high school, I had dreaded a two-pager. Now *National Geographic* magazine wanted me to write about my walk across America, something that had taken me more than a year and a half. I was supposed to be putting all of this down on paper for probably the most prestigious magazine in the USA, a magazine that went to millions of homes throughout the world. I was scared but would try.

During the day I would try to work off my excess energy by running six or seven miles. While jogging I'd think about what adventure from my walk I wanted to write about that night. I also tried to figure out the rather strange environment I now found myself living in. On this *very* quiet campus were more than six hundred men studying to be Baptist ministers and about sixty women studying to be something in Christian work other than ministers. Most would marry ministers or go into Christian education. It was all Greek to me.

The students at the seminary studied some rather strange subjects, I thought. They used words like *exegesis* when they spoke of their classes. They'd say, "Should I take the Exegesis of Isaiah this term or that Survey of the Minor Prophets: Micah and Nahum?" I'd been a Christian for less than two weeks and having always been someone who wanted to find something funny about almost everything, I really had to restrain myself. I thought of all kinds of jokes about Nahum and Micah, whoever they were. Wanting to tell jokes made me feel guilty since God seemed like He should be a very serious subject. And I *was* as serious about my newly admitted faith as I'd ever been about anything in my life.

Some students were studying Greek. The only Greek I knew anything about was the Greek restaurant near where I'd grown up. Others would talk about their Hebrew professor. I didn't think Christians would be studying a language that was Jewish! It's startling to me now to realize how little I knew about Christianity then.

One of the first guys I met on campus was a dark-haired, first-year student named Wally Hebert. He had been born and raised in Cajun country and had a wife named Brenda from Bogalusa, Louisiana, and a two-year-old daughter, Andrea. They were very proud of the fact that Andrea could already speak so well, and as a joke I would always talk to Andrea in wild baby talk. He already had a bachelor's and master's degree in history. Wally didn't look like all the others on campus. Southern Baptist ministers-to-be looked a lot alike to me, just like the young executives at IBM look alike.

Wally had an excellent stereo system that he'd gotten when he served in the Army in Korea. Wally had a surprising collection of record albums—Joni Mitchell; Crosby, Stills, Nash and Young; and Cat Stevens. I assumed that someone at a seminary would not listen to anything but holy organ music. Anyway, Wally loved all kinds of "good" music, from the great hymns in the Baptist hymnal, to Bach's best, to bluegrass and Dixieland jazz. He also introduced me to a style called "contemporary Christian music" where excellent musicians sang ballads, tore off electric guitar licks, and so on. Their lyrics, though, were very different because they talked about Jesus. At the seminary I often felt like I was living in a different country.

Every night before I would start writing I'd go over to Wally and Brenda's apartment on campus to listen to music and drink Wally's Cajun coffee. It was such strong coffee that the first few nights after I drank it I could not get to sleep, at all. The stuff was so potent it should have required a doctor's prescription.

At about 10 P.M., I'd leave the security and softness of their little family and go back to the bleakness of my room in the dorm and write. I had nothing but a metal desk, my backpack in the closet, and my dark red sleeping bag spread out on the bed. I had no idea if what I was writing was any good, but I was becoming totally consumed by what I was doing. A few nights I'd look up from the papers scattered on the desk and notice the room becoming lighter. Through the window I saw the sun coming up.

More and more I felt that the article was something God wanted me to write. I would be able to tell millions of people about the great and inspiring country I'd discovered. And, just as importantly, I hoped to tell them about my search for God and what it had meant to me to become a Christian.

I had learned that *National Geographic* had almost ten million subscribers and that each magazine was read by three to four people. One day one of the more gung ho seminary students said, "Just think, Peter, if you write about your being born again in that magazine, you could witness to almost 40 million people. Think of how long it would take me to preach to that many!"

The month the editors had given me to write quickly passed. One day a call came from Washington.

"Peter, how is your writing coming?" Tom Smith asked. I could hear the soft hiss of the long distance line.

"I'm only about half done," I said, nervous that he would tell me to forget ever writing the article myself. They had once mentioned that if I could not do the writing they would send down an editor to draw the story out of me.

"Well, how much longer do you think it will take, Peter?"

I wanted to tell him I would have it done in a week, but since I'd become a Christian, I felt it was important to tell the truth, regardless.

"It may take quite a while longer, maybe a month." There was no immediate response.

"We really need to see it as soon as you can get it up here." Another moment of tense silence passed as I thought about what to say. "Listen, Peter, what scene are you writing about now?"

"I'm about finished with the part about the black family I lived with in North Carolina."

"When you finish that part, why don't you get it typed up and send it to me. Okay?" Tom sounded upbeat.

"All right, sounds good." We hung up. Standing in the strangely quiet hall of the almost sterile dorm, I felt a million miles away from the world of big-time magazine publishing and had serious doubts about being able to write anything worthy of making it into print anywhere, much less in the *National Geographic*.

By this time I'd met one of the female students at the seminary. Her name was Barbara Pennell, and she seemed too beautiful to be a student at such a place. I asked if she would do some typing for me and she said she would. It took her a week of nights to get it done, although I got the feeling that she was probably too busy studying for her master's degree to be doing this extra work. Could she be interested in me? I was too consumed with my writing to find out, *now*.

My manuscript, neatly double-spaced on an IBM Selectric typewriter, *looked* good, but would the editors like it? I was stuffing the article in a padded envelope when Barbara said, "Peter, I think it would be a good idea for you to have a copy made. I'd be glad to take you to a copy center." That was a good idea.

I put my original, hand-written pages and the typed pages in a file folder and we headed off in Barbara's VW. About halfway there I looked in the back seat to see if the wind was blowing the pages around. I didn't see the file. *Where was it?* I bent my body in half looking on the floor under the seats. I could see nothing. I told Barbara to pull over. We looked some more and saw nothing, *nothing, NOTHING!* Panic ran wild inside of me.

"Where could it be?" Barbara asked, trying to appear relaxed.

"I don't know! I opened the car door for you when we left campus. Then I got in and we drove off."

"Could you have put the papers on top of the car when you opened the door for me?"

"Oh, *no!* That's what I did! Quick, let's drive back and see if we can find them." We were on the interstate, and I pictured all of my precious writing blown away, trampled by semitrucks.

We started driving back to the dorm. Just at the brick columns at the entrance to the campus, a gust of wind picked up a pile of papers and blew them out in front of a smoking city bus. My heart jumped inside my chest until I saw it was just a newspaper. We drove very slowly down the main street of the seminary. I saw nothing. Surely, if the folder had blown off, it would have left the roof of the car before we went far! I was mad at myself for keeping too close an eye on Barbara and not being careful enough with these most precious papers. *Why, God, would You let this happen?* I thought. I was mad at Him, myself, and the whole world. I told Barbara I wanted to be alone, and as I walked toward my room, I sank to the depths of hopelessness.

"Hey, Bro," came a voice I recognized. It was Welch Hill, a friend and student who lived down the hall from me. Welch was not a typical Baptist. He'd grown up as a military brat and had moved all over the USA and spent time in Europe. Welch had also been exposed to the "Jesus Freak" movement out in California. Before he'd become a Christian he had experienced "the world," as devout Christians called things like drug use, dancing, rock music, partying, fast cars, etc.

"What's wrong with you, Peter?" Welch asked.

"You're not going to believe this, but I've lost the manuscript I've been writing for *National Geographic.* Everything." My heart sank to my toes.

"That can't be, Bro."

"It is..."

Welch opened his Bible. The leather cover was worn on the edges. "Pete, I've felt led to share something with you for about a week now, but knowing you've only been a Christian for such a short time I questioned whether I should. You're not supposed to feed meat to a baby Christian. What I want to share with you from the Word is solid meat." He flipped to the back of the Bible.

"Listen to this," Welch went on. " 'For we do not wrestle against flesh and blood, but against principalities, against powers, against the rulers of the darkness of this age, against spiritual hosts of wickedness in the heavenly places.' " I felt the buzz of pure truth, but I didn't understand all of it.

"This means that it's entirely possible that your losing this manuscript has something to do with the battle that's taking place in life between good and evil, God and satan," Welch said. "That's why this Scripture says that we don't fight flesh and blood but we battle powers and rulers of the darkness. This is getting exciting, Pete!" He closed his Bible.

"You know, I've noticed that when God's getting ready to do great things in my life, the powers of the darkness really intensify their war against me."

"Do you really think the article will turn up?" I asked, reaching for any touch of hope.

Welch was silent as a candle. "I believe the Lord has shown me that something great's going to happen with that article of yours. It'll turn up."

Days passed. I so wanted to believe what Welch had said. A week went by. I seriously began to doubt what he'd said. That spiritual warfare stuff was hard for me to grasp fully. I thought all I had to do was become a Christian and that would be all I needed.

Two weeks passed. Nothing. On a quiet and humid afternoon at the dorm the phone rang. Everyone was in classes, and I was afraid to answer. My fears were justified; it was Tom Smith from *National Geographic.*

"Peter, I've been in Central America and I expected to come back and find your manuscript. Where is it? People can't wait much longer here."

"I've had some problems, but you should have it any day." I'd been writing some of the other adventures on the walk.

"This won't wait much longer. I can't make many more excuses," Tom said before hanging up.

Another week passed. One day I was sitting out on the front steps. Welch came in from class and sat down next to me. "What have you been writing about lately?"

"Last night I wrote about my salvation at the James Robison Crusade. Man, it's powerful! But it'll never get published if something doesn't happen."

The paperboy rode toward us on the sidewalk. He pulled in and stopped in front of us. "Are you Peter Jenkins?" the boy asked, shyly. He had freckles.

"Yes, I am."

"My mom's a student here, and she heard talk that you lost some papers. Well, I think I was the one who picked them up."

He turned very red. I knew what he'd say next—that he'd thrown them away. And that's about what he did say.

"I found 'em deliverin' my papers a few weeks ago and brought 'em home. I saw they wasn't nothing but typing and writing and threw them in the wastepaper basket by the sofa." This was almost as hard for him as it was for me.

"So, why are you telling me this?" I asked with shrill tones of temper in my voice.

"Because, my mama looked by the sofa and saw this under it." He pulled the folder out of his paper bag. I wanted to hug the boy, but first I looked inside and everything looked like it was there. He rode off. It turned out the boy had thrown the folder toward the waste can, like a typical twelve year old, but missed and didn't bother to pick it up, figuring his mother would do it. Fortunately, the mother hadn't seen the folder because it had slid under the sofa.

"PRAISE THE LORD!" Welch shouted. I walked to the copy machine with him that day and mailed the manuscript to Washington.

A week later, Tom called and said the editors thought I had potential as a writer but that the story needed a lot of editing. They gave it to one of their editors who was dying of bone cancer. He read it on vacation in the Caribbean islands somewhere and said that there were some diamonds in this rough, really rough writing but he didn't think it was worth all the work.

Then another man named Harvey Arden said he'd give it a shot. Harvey was a caption writer and, in my opinion, a creative genius. Maybe he could do something. About six months passed. Barbara and I got married, then one day we got a call from Tom Smith. He said that *National Geographic* would like to fly us up to Washington, that Harvey had done a masterful job of editing, and they thought, finally, that the article *might* get in the magazine. I was thrilled.

And so here we were in Washington. Harvey brought us to his office and handed me a copy of what he had edited. It looked like Harvey had cut out more than half of what I'd written. The article was about forty-two pages long. I scanned it quickly, sure that I would find my Christian testimony cut out. It wasn't. I was very surprised.

For a week we went through the more than twenty thousand pictures I'd taken. I was super excited working with such powerfully talented people. I tried to soak in everything they said and did. Their chief concern was how many pages the article would be. Every page in *National Geographic* was very precious since a single page of advertising at that time could cost about $75,000. First, they said my article would be forty pages; then they cut it back to thirty-four. Then they shifted another longer story into the same issue and my article dropped down to thirty-two pages. Cutting all those pages would be a tough job for someone and torture for me.

Harvey was asked to make the final cut. He worked late one night and the next morning. When I read his final cuts, I saw that it had finally happened—my Christian testimony was out. At first I was mad and I wanted to make a scene. I thought I should go to someone higher than Harvey and tell him how important this episode was to me and my story. But, I felt the inspiration just to keep quiet. Barbara said, "Let the Lord work this out. If it's meant to be in the magazine, it will be."

The next day Tom invited us to a special luncheon in our honor in the magazine's exclusive dining room. All of the most important people on the magazine staff were there. Special *National Geographic* china settings were elegantly placed, and a butler seated everyone.

Some made small talk as the server brought out the first course. "Well Peter, how's the walk going?" asked Gil Grosvenor, the editor of the magazine.

"Just fine," I said. I told a few stories of the wild and

varied adventures as we ate. I was filled with enthusiasm about the inspiring people and country that I'd found.

"Tell me, Peter," asked Joe Judge, the man in charge of all written parts of the magazine, "what is the most important thing that's happened to you on this walk?" I couldn't tell if he was making conversation or really wanted to know.

"This may sound surprising to you, Joe, but I would have to say that the most important thing that's happened to me is that I became a Christian."

"*Really*," Joe said, possibly caught a bit by surprise at my answer. Barbara kicked me under the table as a show of support, as if to say "Sic 'em."

"Harvey," Joe asked, "is this in Peter's article?"

"No, we had to cut back to thirty-two pages, so I took it out." No one said it, but I knew that many on the staff considered my conversion to Christianity potentially controversial.

"Well, if it means that much to Peter, I think we need to put it back in. Can we get a couple more pages, Gil?"

"I think so, Joe," he answered. The article was increased from thirty-two to thirty-four pages, and my salvation experience appeared in *National Geographic* magazine.

As we walked back to the hotel that evening, Barbara said, "You know, honey, God really works in mysterious ways." I was learning fast that I had so much to learn about His ways.

"For My thoughts are not your thoughts,
Nor are your ways My ways,"
    says the LORD.
For as the heavens are higher than the earth,
So are My ways higher than your ways,
And My thoughts than your thoughts.
                    Isaiah 55:8–9

10

The Lady and the Lincoln Continental

We had been on the road one year. Today was Peter's twenty-sixth birthday, July 8, 1977. We moved slowly westward, headed into the open wilds of Texas. The sun blistered and baked us, turning us as red as the clay we walked on. The land was lean, cracked by dry and gusty wind, crying out for moisture.

Peter appeared a little depressed—his birthday just another day on the road. This was one of the few times I ever saw a hint of self-pity in him, and I was secretly glad. Somehow, his "blue" mood made all my emotional upheavals seem more acceptable; my strong and daring husband was not made out of stone but was capable of feelings, too. I knew all about Peter's strength and fearlessness. What I yearned to know more about was the deep inner feelings he guarded like the Pentagon guards its secrets. My only clues to what was going on inside Peter came through his anger when he would spout off or explode.

We walked past a man who was feeding his cattle outside his ranch house. He looked up and watched us, curi-
ously. His huge silver belt buckle sparkled in the blazing sun.
Peter and I had noticed that people were becoming more
open and friendly the farther west we walked. They were
open, like the land they lived on. The rancher tilted back his
wide-brimmed cowboy hat, wiped his brow, and said, "Don't
know which is hotter, what yer doin' or what I'm doin'!"
There was humor in his voice.

We lifted our hands and waved. It was too hot to stop.

"Have a big time now!" he yelled and went back to
feeding his cows.

Not many miles farther a man drove up to us in his car
and stopped. He was alone, and we recognized him right
away. His name was Jim Bob Nation, a middle-aged man
we'd met in a café a few days ago. He was an insurance sales-
man and ran a small business in Azle, Texas. He had driven
out to find us and stepped out of his car with a big smile on
his face.

"Couldn't let ya get clean away without wishin' ya a
happy birthday," Jim Bob said to Peter.

"How did you know it was my birthday?" Peter asked.

"Read it in the *Geographic*," Jim Bob answered.

We had forgotten that Peter's birth date was in the *National Geographic* article, which had finally been accepted
and published the previous April. We were constantly
amazed at the number of people who had read the story or
now knew of Peter Jenkins and his walk across America. Peter often went unrecognized, however, because he was always
associated with his dog Cooper. And the general public did
not know he was married and had a woman on the road with
him.

Peter's eyes lit up and a smile broke his somber expression. Jim Bob pulled out a big basket and flipped open a table
cloth. He spread out a picnic of fried chicken, home-canned

pickles, cantaloupe, tomatoes, bread, cold Cokes, and lemon cake for Peter's birthday. Although Jim Bob lived alone, he was a good cook and had prepared this meal by himself. We ate, rested, and had a special birthday party for Peter alongside the hot road. It was as though a personal messenger had been sent to bring birthday cheer and let Peter know he had not been forgotten in the middle of Texas. Jim Bob gave us each a pencil with his name on it and bid us a safe and happy journey.

When the sun dropped behind the horizon like a big ball, we found a grassy, level spot to pitch our tent in a cow pasture, under a mesquite tree, the perfect ending to a birthday. The evening winds began to cool the earth and stars filled the heavens. The only sounds were the bawls of calves and an occasional hoot from an owl. Quietness enfolded us and we felt at peace with the world. We slept like royalty in the grass, the hardened cow patties underneath our tent a perfect mattress, our rolled-up T-shirts, perfect pillows.

In what seemed seconds it was sunrise, 6:30 A.M., and time to get up. I wasn't ready and rolled over on my rubber mat to catch a few more winks.

My eyes half-opened, I thought I saw something looking into the tent. My contact lenses were still in the case, so I wasn't sure what was giving me the eye. I pulled back the flap and grabbed for my glasses.

"Peter!" I screamed.

He woke up with a jolt.

Standing in front of us, peering into our little tent door, was the biggest bull I had ever seen. He was so close I could smell his breath. He snorted. His horns looked ten feet long and the width of his head filled the opening. His was the ugliest face I had ever seen, with or without my glasses.

Peter hustled to his feet, scrambling for his walking shorts, reaching for anything to throw at the bull. Peter cleared his throat and, drawing on his best repertoire of cow moos, bellowed out a bull call. The bull stepped back. He was far enough away for Peter to reach outside the tent door and grab a stick. He threw it at the bull. The massive animal stepped back again, reluctantly, and stared.

"Get out of here!" Peter yelled in his fiercest tones. The bull turned and sauntered away.

Several days later we were leaving Olney, a little west Texas town where we had stopped. Folks in Olney had been good to us. In this small town, word of our arrival had travelled fast, and most of the townsfolk knew who we were. Several had even asked us into their homes for meals.

During our brief stay we had attended a community celebration for the Olney bank, seen a baseball game, and watched a handicapped man named Asa Pease make beautiful leather belts. The local newspaper had written a feature story, "National Geographic Hikers Are Here," which was supposed to be in today's paper. But we were on our way again and would only read it if someone mailed a copy to us up the road.

Six miles out of town we were approaching Ben's and Louise's B.B.Q. Cafe, recommended by everyone in Olney.

"Cain't miss it. It's on yer way out of town and the food's larrupin' good," people had told us. "Best barbecue anywheres."

It was almost noon and a perfect time to eat. A big barbecue sandwich sounded great. We dropped our backpacks outside in the shade and went inside. Two picnic tables for seating customers were in the middle of the one room café, and a man stood behind the counter. Peter gave him our order and we sat on a bench, anticipating this good food.

Before our order was ready, an older woman barged through the café door. She was dressed in a stylish suit, and her gray hair, which had just been fixed, was stiff with hair spray. Heavy makeup plastered over her western, leathery skin made her look much younger than her years. She looked very rich and important and had a brassy, intimidating air.

The woman gave the café owner her orders for carry-out barbecue, talking to him as if he were a personal servant. Her tone was clipped, "no nonsense and hurry up." She turned to us and looked Peter over, then looked me up and down.

"What are you, a girl?" she asked me, arrogantly. This scene apparently gave her pleasure.

True, my hair was pushed under my floppy hat, I wore no makeup, my legs were muscular, I wore outdoor gear, and I had on a big pair of boots. But there was no way to mistake me for a man at this close range. I burned with anger. Her words stung, bringing back painful memories of how I'd struggled over my identity, the loss of femininity on the walk, and being misunderstood by most women who saw me on the road.

Everything inside me screamed at her. Never in my life had I wanted to beat up a person, but I did now. As I swallowed the knot in my throat and thought wildly about how to respond to this older woman's cruel insult, she walked over to me, placed her hand on my shoulder, and pulled me around. My body tingled with disbelief, as she pulled and pushed me like a bully.

"Yep, you're a girl," she snickered.

I was shocked and couldn't think. Older people were not supposed to act like this, and I was supposed to treat my elders with respect! I had never been particularly talented at witty "comebacks," so all I said was, "Some people in this world are crude."

This didn't faze her, and she acted as though she hadn't heard me. She might not have since my voice was so low and shaky with emotion.

The woman grabbed her order from the owner. I noted that she had been served before us. She clutched her sacks of food and turned her nose upward as she walked by. She opened the door and darted a haughty look back at us.

"Do you all want to borrow my Lincoln Continental instead of walking?" she asked with a hoity-toity smirk.

"If we had wanted to ride, we would have used our Rolls Royce at home," Peter said.

The temperature climbed past one hundred degrees every day, hot enough to melt a candle. To shade us from the unforgiving sun, we had attached giant golfing umbrellas to our backpacks. The umbrellas were the brainstorm of a friend of ours, Shelley Mayfield, a professional golfer. We had met him during our stay in Dallas, and he had encouraged us to use these wide umbrellas for shade since there would be no trees where we were headed. We looked like Mary Poppins as we plugged along through range land that only rattlesnakes, coyotes, and horned toads call home. Occasionally, we passed some Texas longhorn steers who stared at us as much as we stared at them.

One day a Texas sheriff in a brown Plymouth pulled up next to us. A big cigar hung from the corner of his mouth, and his face was round with fat cheeks. I could see his stomach touching the steering wheel inside his car. We couldn't imagine what he wanted; *another curious person*, we thought. He rolled down his window, and I felt a blast of cold air from the air conditioning. He smiled. "Where ya headed in this heat?" he asked.

"We're walking across the USA," I answered since I was closer to him.

His cigar fell to the tip of his lips in shock as he looked at me and gulped.

"At least you got a stout pair o' legs on ya! Bet yer a corn-fed country girl."

"You bet!" I laughed.

We gave him some post cards to mail for us in the next town. He said his name was Bennie Taylor, a sergeant of police. He drove off shaking his head.

With September around the corner, soon it would be getting cooler and we would not have to endure the draining heat much longer. Another day was ending as we hiked north on a back road in the Texas Panhandle. I felt like a sheet of sandpaper, covered with grit and dirt. Since I covered my face each morning with Vaseline, my skin acted like flypaper, catching all the bugs and sand blown around by the hot wind. Night was already falling and we had not found a campsite. We had just crossed a barren stretch, fifteen miles of nothing but desert and sagebrush, and were hoping to stop near enough to Quanah, Texas, so that we could have breakfast the next morning without having to walk five to ten miles.

Right at dark we passed a house trailer. Loud music poured from a stereo, and some young men walked in and out of the front door. They wore blue jeans and open shirts and had long hair. They carried cans of beer. It looked like a party was going on; maybe a drug party. A car with its headlights on passed us slowly and turned into the driveway. Hollering and laughing could be heard from the road. I was becoming frightened but didn't want to tell Peter. My mind raced and my feet hurried to catch up with Peter who was ahead of me and I couldn't see him very well in the dark. We never walked after dark, it was just too dangerous. But here we were in the middle of open range, just us and the wild party. What if we were discovered by these half-drunk or drugged men? Anything could happen. I'd seen lots of movies where people were threatened, kidnapped, robbed, raped, killed, and never heard from again. One long-haired man stood at the door and stared out toward us. I couldn't tell if he could see us or not.

"Excuse me, but may I be curious for a moment?" came a voice out of the blackness. I jumped like I had been shot and thought I'd die on the spot. The voice was such a surprise that my heart nearly stopped. At least Peter was just a few steps ahead of me.

It was hard to see and I had no idea there was a person on the side of the road next to us. The voice was that of an older man. "My wife, Iva Mae, and I were sitting out in the backyard and we saw you coming from way off before dark. We were wondering what you were doing. We knew you had some kind of purpose because of your backpacking gear. We knew you weren't just out hitchhiking or bums."

The man introduced himself as Leroy Gibson and he lived across the road. It was so dark we had not seen his house. His place was not far from the trailer.

"We live here on the edge of town just a couple miles out of Quanah," he said.

Only minutes after I feared we might be tortured or murdered by wild-eyed dope fiends, we found ourselves sitting in lawn chairs, drinking iced tea, talking about our walk across America with a sweet couple about the age of our parents. The light from the back porch shone and we could see their faces. Leroy had black hair touched with gray, and Iva Mae had the whitest, purest skin I'd seen since New Orleans. Her eyes were clear blue and deep. Their quiet gentleness made us feel safe and secure. We talked for a couple of hours and learned that Leroy was a rural route mailman and that Iva Mae worked at the First National Bank in Quanah. They had two grown sons, Mike who was a doctor, and Ridley, a banker. Leroy talked with pride about his sons and their families, their accomplishments and, especially, how glad he was that they were vital Christians.

This was a refreshing change from the recent experience with the brassy woman at the barbecue café, and a welcome refuge from the trailer party down the road. Before our conversation ended, Leroy and Iva Mae invited us to sleep in their spare bedroom, go to church with them, and speak to their young people's group at the First Baptist Church. They asked us to attend a baptismal service with them at Copper Breaks State Park where their pastor, Forrest Sheffield, would be taking seven converts down under the water.

Of course. We would love to be a part of all they had asked us to do with them. All of this had happened before any of us had taken a daylight look at one another.

Trust in Him at all times, you people;
Pour out your heart before Him;
God is a refuge for us.

Psalm 62:8

11

"Hey! Peat-ah"

This was going to be a day of miracles but I had yet to see them. We were still in Texas. At times I thought we would spend the rest of our lives walking across this state.

Heading northwest on Highway 87, we were inching our way to the border and were almost to New Mexico. We had passed several ponds speckled with ducks and geese that were en route to winter nests in the south. Cool winds were blowing from the north, and we were racing to make the mountains of Colorado before winter set in. We had several hundred miles to walk before we got to those mountains and this was late September.

We had covered seventeen miles the day before and today I was dragging. My body didn't want to go. Whenever I lifted my head, all I could see was barren ranch land, flat, open, and forever. This was one of those days I wished I was someone else, somewhere else, and certainly doing something besides walking with thirty pounds on my back. No matter how many times I told myself to "Praise God in all things," I was a long way from praising anything. I watched the ground. This was less depressing than looking into the vast horizon and realizing I still had all that space to cover on foot.

Peter and I talked little. He usually stayed hundreds of yards ahead of me, taking pictures, watching, observing the environment, and dreaming big dreams. We had come a long way from New Orleans, in more ways than miles. We were fighting less and less. I was more adjusted to the rigors of the walk, and Peter was more tolerant of my inability to match his pace. I had learned to save my energy for making miles instead of quarrels.

I lifted one heavy boot after the other. I became mesmerized by the steady, continuous motion of my feet. Hour after hour. A lizard wiggled through the grass as I passed by; then a few steps further, I watched a black, wooly tarantula mosey across the road. After hundreds of miles I had learned that most creatures were more afraid of me than I was of them. Seldom did I jump anymore at the sight of them. It took too much energy, and I needed every ounce of strength to keep moving.

We were almost to the New Mexico border but I was dragging far behind, partly because I had not eaten all day— nothing substantial, that is, a few nuts and one apple. We purposely did not carry pots, pans, and lots of food because of the added weight. We usually carried fruit, sometimes bread and canned meat, nuts, raisins, and crackers, enough to last two or three days between towns. But our most precious resource was water, which weighed about eight pounds per gallon, and that was more important than food. We were almost to Texline and would be able to eat there. Yet, I didn't feel like I was going to make it.

This was Tuesday, September 20, 1977. Eighteen more miles before we could eat. About eight hours from now. "Hey...Peter. Gotta stop...Need rest," I yelled faintly.

Peter looked back and stopped. He knew today was a rough one for me and he wasn't pushing. We were walking along railroad tracks bordered by patches of shrubbery. I needed to go to the bathroom and gratefully spotted a tall shrub to hide behind. Although we were in a desolate area my modesty was always with me. As I slipped down a mound beside the track, a peculiar feeling rippled through me.

Peter walked back to where I had dumped my backpack, unloaded his pack, and sat down for a rest. I stumbled toward the bush, aware that my vision wasn't as sharp through my thick glasses. My contact lenses were packed away since I couldn't wear them in the dry, dusty air. The unusual feeling came back. The thought *snake* flitted through my mind. It seemed as though something had told me to watch out for a snake.

I heard the rattles just as I approached the big bush. There, curled up and ready to strike, was the widest, roundest, fattest rattlesnake I had ever seen. I screamed.

"Rattlesnake! Rattlesnake!" I shouted as I turned and ran as fast as I could back to Peter.

Peter ran by me with a big rock. The snake had slithered through the brush and onto the railroad tracks when Peter caught up to it. The rattler curled up again, ready to strike. Peter picked up a large chunk of metal and threw it at the snake. The snake jumped, hissing and rattling. Peter hurled the rock. Then another rock. Again. Peter was a good shot and stunned the snake. He crept close and beat its head into the rails. The rattlesnake had eight rattles on its tail and was at least five feet long.

This ordeal nearly finished me off, taking a toll on my already weakened body. We left the railroad tracks and got back on the deserted highway and moved at a snail's pace. We were five miles from town. No way was I going to make it. The sun was sinking and five miles was like fifty to me. Peter was several block lengths ahead of me. I staggered like a drunk. My ankles turned, and I nearly fell every other step. My shoulders were slumped, and I was about to collapse when a brown car passed us going so slow that I could read the Louisiana license plates.

"Peat-ah. Peat-ah." I heard a woman holler. There was no mistaking the accent. It was "Nu-Awlins" for sure.

"Hey...Peat-ah. Can ya believe it?" She screamed with laughter. "It's me, Rita."

Rita Hauptman and her brother, Teddy, from New Orleans jumped from the car and came running to us. Rita was a small, slightly plump woman in her late fifties with short, cropped hair and glasses. She was the kind of person who seemed to be joking and laughing all the time but was serious about life. She lived alone, having been divorced for many years, and her family was grown. She spent most of her time operating a flower and gift shop in New Orleans or traveling with her brother who lived in the same building as her shop. Rita and Teddy took trips every year, touring the USA. Teddy was a businessman, shrewd and dollar-wise. He had snow-white hair and was a tall, heavy man with a raspy voice from a lifetime of smoking. Teddy appeared rough, but down deep, buried under a thick crust, was another person. He liked scoffing at Rita about her constant church attendance.

Rita attended the Word of Faith Temple where Peter and I had been married. She was a charter member of the church and had been in the congregation the day Peter and I heard the sermon, "Will You Go with This Man?" She had been interested in us without our knowing it at the time, and before we left New Orleans, she became our main link with the church by sending us tapes and bulletins from the services.

"God wants me to be your prayer warrior, and I'm going to pray for you every single day you are on this walk. You got a tape recorder? Get one, cause you need to hear the Word of God while you're out there." She had a straightforward and no-nonsense way of talking.

Peter carried a small tape recorder in his pack. She

sent her packages to general delivery at the small-town post offices we passed through.

We had become good friends with this little woman through her letters and tapes. One of her letters stood out in my memory. It would have shocked me earlier in my life, but since I had experienced some extraordinary things in the last couple of years, I appreciated what she had to say.

> Dear Pete and Barb,
>
> I have something to tell you. About two weeks ago, I saw a picture of you in my mind, walking, completely disappearing in Christ...He seemed to be with you walking, then engulfing you till I saw only Him. I never mentioned it or thought about it as it seemed I had dreamed it. Then last week, the same thing happened. I wish you could see it. It's so real. Jesus...Dusty...Opening the way...Not leading but opening...It's hard to explain, but believe me it's not imagination. You are still daily in my prayers and I wait patiently to hear. Ted always asks how much longer will it take you to finish. Take care of each other.
>
> Rita.

"What a kick. What a kick!" Rita cried and giggled as she hugged us, her short, plump body bouncing with laughter. Teddy ran round the other side of the car and embraced me.

"I told Rita the little guy walking in the back had just about had it. I never dreamed it was you!" Teddy said to me. He was as excited as Rita.

"You won't believe this," Rita said. "We've been on vacation out West and have talked about yous two for the past eight days, hoping by some crazy chance to see yous on the road...And you'll never guess what happened."

"Never made a wrong turn in my life," Teddy interrupted. "Never missed a road on a map, but we missed our turn and were so far down this highway, we decided to keep going until we came to the interstate."

"And we saw these two hikers. And would ya believe it was Peat-ah and Bah-bra...What a kick!" Rita laughed.

"One chance in a million," Teddy said.

"Are yas hungry?" Rita asked. Meanwhile, Teddy was unlocking the trunk of the car.

"Would ya believe we just stopped at the last town and filled up our trunk with food?" Teddy said.

Teddy started pulling out food faster than we could handle it—milk, jugs of orange juice, cookies, Cracker Jacks, Cokes—more food than we had seen in days.

My body was aching tired, but my heart almost burst with gladness. Rita and Teddy had no way of knowing how desperately I needed this food, this moment, their laughter, their hugs. Out of nowhere they had come. By chance? I was beginning to believe that nothing happened by chance anymore.

Soon I was pumped up with new energy and motivation. Rita was so thrilled she wanted to walk the rest of the way into town with us, another five miles. Teddy drove ahead in the car to find a motel for all of us. Rita talked and jabbered and filled our ears with news from New Orleans and Word of Faith and how Teddy was still fighting the Lord, but that God had surely spoken to him today since he made the wrong turn and then found us alongside the road.

At dusk Rita, Peter, and I reached the little town of Texline. Teddy met us, puffing from shortness of breath, and took my backpack to lighten my load.

"Let's get some suppa," Teddy said, pointing to a café ahead.

We unloaded our packs in the motel rooms Teddy had paid for. I wanted to take a quick bath and clean up before we ate. I noticed that Peter had dropped his backpack and some of his gear in the bathroom before hurrying outside to help Teddy unload the car. Just as I was about to turn on the water, I noticed Peter's empty water bottle in the tub and a little gray shadow underneath. Peter had forgotten to tell me. Thank God, I was too tired to be jumpy. There, nestled in the bottom of the tub, was a baby prairie rattler, more deadly than any adult rattlesnake. Peter had been carrying it in his empty water bottle since early this morning when he found it curled up next to his hiking boots beside the tent. He said he wanted to examine it more closely since he'd never seen one before.

I would bathe later.

For He satisfies the longing soul,
And fills the hungry soul with goodness.

Psalm 107:9

12

Two Odd Couples

Colorado, Colorado, here we come! We could feel the pull of the Rocky Mountains and knew we had to get to the heart of them. We were on Highway 56 between Clayton and Springer, New Mexico, almost a hundred mile stretch of open grasslands and chilly winds. The land was preparing for a dramatic change from flat range to the majestic Rockies as we looked across a span of nearly fifty miles and could see peaks through the clouds. Those knots were the tops of mountains, the mighty Rocky Mountains. We were sure that some of those peaks were across the border in Colorado, but we had a long way yet to go.

The quietness of this land felt so good. No traffic. No stores, cafés, houses, cars, buildings, no nothing. Mile after mile of openness with the wonderful exception of herds of antelope. They were everywhere, watching us and loping across the plains. Their tan hides blended with the tall grass but the white stripes across their heads and tails made them visible from the road. They resembled graceful ballerinas as they pranced, skipped, and bounded through the fields. I felt as though I were in the finest theater in the world, watching an opera set to the music of the wind.

As Peter and I marvelled at the lovely creatures, they must have marvelled at us, too. How odd we must have looked to them, strange, two-legged creatures invading their world. As we walked in solitude for many hours, the antelope danced along with us from a distance. A group of eight moved parallel to us about a quarter mile from the road, but one pair, a buck and a doe, ventured closer. They were young and flirtatious. They would gallop toward us, then slam to a stop before getting too close. Peter and I took off our packs and grabbed our cameras, all the while talking to them in a soothing voice. They were curious and stared at us as if we were from another planet, but just as we stepped to within ten feet of them, they would leap straight up into the air and dart off. Back and forth, they teased us, coming close and then running away. We understood them and their interest in us and wished we could touch them. They were so much like us, male and female, full of life and energy and love, discovering their world. The couple walked beside us for at least a mile, as if they wanted to share some moments of our walk across America and provide us with some encouragement.

Later the same day we stopped at a windmill to get some water. Water was very scarce on the open range and at the windmills we usually had to shove the cattle away to fill our water bottles. The constant wind blowing across the plains kept the water flowing into the big round water tubs from the pipe that stuck out of the ground. Good, clean, cold water. The cows looked at us like we had cut in line in front of them, but they shared their water with us without complaint. Our water bottles filled, we were set for the rest of the day and night.

On the road again, walking toward the northwest, we felt a magnet was drawing us toward Colorado. We knew we needed to hole up there for winter, but we still didn't know where we would stop. Peter and I had not discussed it. It was one of those things that was a little touchy, not worth arguing or worrying about. "We'll just make it to Colorado before snowfall and everything will be all right," Peter had said.

Make it there in the next few weeks? Sure! Sure! I thought. My faith had increased the past year and a half on the road, but I still felt edgy about where we would stay for the whole winter. You didn't just walk into the Rocky Mountains, pitch a tent in eighty feet of snow, and bake cookies all winter. And you didn't just walk into a mountain village, without a job or money, and rent a furnished apartment. Out there in the middle of New Mexico, on the open plains, the answer came.

We had moved several miles past the windmill when a late-model car passed us, stopped, and backed up. We didn't know who the passengers were until a man jumped out of the car and walked back to us. It was Jack Gross, and his wife Jerry from Borger, Texas.

"Well, you don't say," Jack said. "Never know who you'll run into on the side of the road these days." He chuckled, sipping something from a glass. Jack was middle-aged, wore glasses, and had black hair and brisk manners. We had met Jack during our stay with Peter's uncle George Robie. Peter's uncle and Jack had both worked together for Phillips Petroleum until Jack decided to go out on his own, wildcatting and drilling for oil himself. Jack grinned at us like an oilman who had struck pay dirt.

"You plan to make it to Colorado before winter?" he asked. We had told Jack and Jerry when we had visited them what our plans were. Now they were on their way to a little mountain town called Lake City, located in the heart of the San Juan Mountains in southwestern Colorado.

"The most beautiful place in the world...I've been to Switzerland and the Alps, and this place, Lake City, beats anything I've ever seen. You know, you all should go there for the winter. In fact, I'll tell my friend, Perk Vickers, yer coming. He has a ranch there, could rent you a cabin, and the whole thing. What do you say?" Jack asked.

No doubt about it, no room for discussion with this Texan. Jack had not struck it rich being idle or afraid to make decisions. "Yep, that's where yer going and I'll tell Perk to get things ready for ya."

Jack and his wife drove off in a hurry, shooting gravel from underneath the back tires. He would be there late to-night, in Lake City, Colorado, to get us a place for the winter. This man, a mere acquaintance to us, this friend of Uncle George...Who would have ever thought our shelter for the winter would be arranged in such a way?

We would not find out until years later what Jack had done for us. Jack never told us himself but we learned that he had made arrangements with Perk Vickers to pay for our lodging that winter in case we didn't have the money.

Peter and I were closer and more in love than ever. Walking together was sheer and absolute joy as we absorbed the beauty around us. The aspens fluttered their golden leaves in the fall sunlight, shimmering and adding glorious color to the mountains. The tall, deep green pines and spruce stood guard over the yellow aspens. Walking fifteen to twenty miles was a breeze, like an afternoon walk in the park, as we crossed the Sangre de Cristo mountain range and dropped down into a valley in southeastern Colorado. We were on Highway 159, moving with ease through the crisp seventy-degree autumn air.

We had walked through places like Wild Horse Mesa, Costilla, and San Luis and were headed toward Ft. Garland. On October 15, 1977, we were so in tune, in such good shape and so exhilarated by the air and the scenery, that we could cover five to seven miles at a time without stopping for a rest. And the nights were cool and brisk, perfect for serious sleep-ing.

Everything was perfect. Almost. Life on the road, like

life anywhere else I suppose, always had one little thorn somewhere and this time it was money. We did have money, but not in our pockets. A money order sent from Don and Sarah Stevens in Dallas awaited us at the post office in Ft. Garland. We had developed such a good friendship with these Texans that they wanted to help us, any way possible. So, we had asked them to become our mailing address and send us money from our banking account whenever we needed it. Most post offices are closed on Saturday, and if they do open, it's only for a few hours in the morning. This was a Saturday afternoon and there was no way to get our money order. It meant we would not have any food to eat until Monday morning when the post office opened.

Our thoughts were mixed with the anxiety over our financial situation and the realization that today was the fourth anniversary of the walk. Four years ago, long before I ever met Peter, he had left Alfred, New York, to begin his journey.

Another thing that nagged at our joy was knowing that today was the opening of elk season and hunters were everywhere. We had to be very careful to stay near the road, otherwise we might be mistaken for an elk and shot. There was a lot to think about. Without ceremony we looked ahead to Ft. Garland and prayed.

At 3:30 in the afternoon a car headed toward us, pulled off to the side, and stopped. It was so filled with suitcases and clothes that it was hard to see the driver and passenger. We waited. Many good things had happened to us when cars stopped so we were not afraid but stayed constantly vigilant.

Don and Doris Jackson rolled down their windows, their faces beaming smiles: more of Uncle George's friends from Borger, Texas. Colorado seemed full of Texans and friends of Uncle George's. Don was a business partner of Jack Gross's, and we had met Don and Doris when we were in Texas. They were on their way home from Breckenridge, Colorado, and had decided to take this scenic back road. Never in a million years did they think they would see us again, much less walking on the road.

We were next to the city limits of Ft. Garland so we agreed to ride in the car with them to a café for something to eat. We always refused to take car rides when we were on the road, but if we were in town we occasionally accepted a ride to a café if someone asked us to eat with him. Then, we always went back to the spot where we'd been picked up and started walking from there again.

Don had invited us, so we knew we wouldn't have to pay the bill. That would fill our stomachs until Monday, when our money would be available at the post office. Peter and I quickly climbed into the front seat with Don and Doris because their car was packed full. We had not bathed for days and our scent was strong in these close quarters. Peter quickly rolled down the window and apologized to Doris for smelling so bad. She laughed and told us not to worry.

By the time we found a café we had filled them in on meeting Jack Gross in New Mexico, our plans to stay in Lake City, and would they mind showing us where the post office was in Ft. Garland? It was on the main corner of town. Peter read the sign telling when the office would open on Monday.

Don's curiosity got the best of him and he asked Peter what we were expecting at the post office. Peter hesitated. Being flat broke was a little embarrassing, and we had a policy never to ask for money or look like we wanted handouts. We never knocked on doors, begged for food, or asked people to help us. We felt that it was our responsibility to take care of ourselves, and if we were in need we should look for ways to meet our needs with God's help.

After Peter hemmed and hawed for about five minutes, he finally told Don we were waiting for some money.

"Well, why didn't you say something sooner?" Don said. "That's no problem." He reached into his wallet and pulled out a bill. He must have sensed our independence and didn't want to offend us. "Now, this is just a loan and you can pay it back when your money comes."

"We really appreciate this," Peter said, looking self-controlled. He put the folded bill in his shorts pocket.

After a happy visit over our meal, Don and Doris had to leave for the long trip back to Borger, so we said our good-byes and watched them pull away. Peter and I lingered over our coffee. We both knew what the other was thinking. Without speaking Peter pulled the money Don had given him out of his pocket. We were both secretly hoping we'd have enough to tide us through the weekend. Peter carefully unfolded the bill. It was a hundred dollars.

Therefore do not worry, saying, "What shall we eat?" "What shall we drink?" or "What shall we wear?" For after all these things the Gentiles seek. For your heavenly Father knows that you need all these things.

Matthew 6:31–32

13

The Slide Show

The day after we arrived in the tiny mountain village of Lake City a blizzard hit. The snow fell in thick swirls and stacked up a foot deep before the day was over. We had just made it.

Peter and I were snuggled into our first home, a two-bedroom cabin with a fireplace. Outside were heaps of aspen logs and black coal to burn and keep us warm. Our cabin sat at about eight thousand feet, overlooking the Vickers' ranch and the headwaters for the Colorado River. It was the most idyllic, heavenly spot I'd ever seen.

We had everything we needed and more. There were a stove, refrigerator, beds, electric blankets, couch, table and chairs—everything. I felt like a mother hen with her nest. I arranged, rearranged, cleaned, puttered over every detail of that cabin to make it home. I made bouquets out of wild weeds, hung our one change of clothes in the closet, and placed crystallized rocks around the room for décor. Before long the cabin was mine.

Perk and Emma Jean Vickers seemed thrilled, too,

that we were on their ranch for the winter. This lovely spot in the high Rockies, located almost sixty miles from the nearest town of any size, could get awfully lonely during a snow-bound winter. Only about a hundred hard-core folks toughed it out here in the winter, and we had joined the group. Nothing could have made me happier; I was more than ready to settle down, be in our own place, and really work on our marriage.

Peter had other ideas. He wanted to work on a book, *A Walk Across America*, a result of the popularity of Peter's article with the same title in *National Geographic*. As snow piled up day after day, we settled in and started writing. Peter wrote at night since he felt more creative then, pecking away with two fingers on our new, used IBM typewriter. We had splurged and bought it knowing the publisher wouldn't accept hard-to-read manuscript typed on a machine with jammed keys.

This was to be Peter's story about his experiences from New York to New Orleans. He had to tell it in his own way, while I acted as editor. Each day I would go over his material—adding, subtracting, retyping, restructuring. Then after he read what I had done, a regular eruption occurred. We had a fight a page.

Peter seemed to want my help but not my interference with his material. I struggled to figure out which was which. Some of my comments and changes he liked, but most of them made him furious, and we would argue for an hour over one or two pages. After a few weeks of this kind of work, I was frustrated to the point of a brawl. We had not yet found a solution to working together.

"That sounds stupid," Peter said. I had just read him an edited page. I had changed a lot of it. "It sounded much better the way I had it written."

"Okay. If you don't like it, then why did you give it to me for my comments?" I answered with a sting.

"Comments, yeah, but not complete changes. This is my book, my story, remember?"

My feelings about helping Peter write were mixed with other frustrations about his story that had come out in the magazine six months earlier. The article had ended with Peter's reaching the Gulf Coast, planting his footprints in the sand, and watching them wash away in the tide. Unfortunately, from my point of view, the ten million subscribers to *National Geographic* had no idea Peter was no longer walking alone, even though we had been married more than a year when the article was published. Even though I had worked by his side on the article. Even though we had been on the road together more than one and a half years.

I had learned through many encounters since the article had been published to swallow my pride and hurt feelings and ignore what people said when they ran into us and met Peter.

"Hey, I read about you in the *National Geographic*. What a story. It sure broke me up when your dog died. Have you got another one yet?" Then the person would notice me. "Where'd ya find her?"

"I picked her up on Bourbon Street," Peter would joke. I would force a smile.

"Well, sure am glad you found somebody to take Cooper's place." Everybody would laugh. "He sure was some dog. It must be exciting to be walking across America. Boy, I could sit and talk to you for hours. What's the most exciting thing that's happened to you? I can't believe I'm talking to the real Peter Jenkins."

And the conversation would go on and on while I stood by, listening to the same stories I'd heard over and over. Most of the time I would find a spot and sit down until Peter had talked himself out. Inside, I was struggling with anger, jealousy, and impatience. I didn't like what I was feeling and tried very hard to cover my emotions. I felt left out, like an afterthought. Surely, this was the untold side of *my* walk across America—my inner anguish, the back seat I took to Peter's adventure although I was very much a part of it.

What was God telling me? What was He trying to teach me? Why was I feeling this way? A lot of sinister and imperfect attitudes were coming to the surface. They needed to be cut out, and I had a long way to go. Whenever I tried to explain to Peter that I felt left out and ignored for my contribution to the article and the walk, he told me I was just looking for something to gripe about.

"Who wants to hear all of your nagging and complaining all the time?" Peter said.

"I'll be glad when you treat me like a wife, instead of a replacement for your dog," I snapped.

As the weeks passed we began to jell together on the book just as we had walking together. We began to tread more softly, watching our sensitive spots, and picking the right moments to discuss writing. Our editor, Pat Golbitz in New York, was happy with what we were sending her and said, "Whatever you are doing, keep doing it." Little did she know all the pain we had been through.

As the book took shape, for diversion Peter learned to trap coyotes in the high country and I tried new recipes. We were making ready for some visitors. Peter's younger brother, Scott, was coming, as was our friend from New Orleans, Welch Hill, who had been an usher in our wedding. I cleaned and baked and made our little cabin as inviting as I could.

Welch was a few years older than Peter, still unmarried and trying to find his niche in life. He was an ex-combat marine-turned-preacher. He had studied at the Baptist seminary while we were there and during the past year he had been working on another religious degree in Anaheim, California. His passion for God and the Bible was great. Because of his disciplined military background he studied the Bible more than anyone I had ever known. When he wrote us a note to tell us he was on his way home to Alabama for Christmas, and could he stop in to see us in Lake City, I felt honored by his words:

> You're really back to Eden these days, trees ...mountains...But not cherubim or flaming sword to bar your way, only an open door that He has opened and no man or demon can shut. The most exciting events lie ahead. Deut 3:5-10. See you soon.
> In Jesus, Welch (saved 8/10/72)

We made new friends in Lake City, like Gary and Jean Wysocki. Gary was a modern day Paul Bunyan, big...*big*...*BIG*. He stood well over six feet, with shoulders as wide as a doorway, a thick head of auburn hair, and a bushy beard that covered most of his face and neck. His eyes were like the Colorado sky, blue and clean. In spite of his massive size, Gary was gentle like one of the high mountain deer. He fit into these mountains, but like everyone else in Lake City, he was struggling to find work and make a living. He and Jean had been married a few years when we met them and ate dinner in their log cabin.

Jean was a Southerner from Mississippi, now a converted mountaineer. She loved Lake City and was not unhappy piling wood into their stove to keep warm in the winter or driving sixty miles one way to fill her cupboards with groceries. Jean was like a flower against the brown cliffs and steep hillsides. With big sparkling eyes, long blond hair, and a beautifully sculptured face, she made a striking mate for the handsome Gary.

Gary and Jean had met when they were both part of a musical group called "Up with People." The group sang and danced and put on shows all over the country and world. Gary was a stage manager and directed the group, making sure the sound and lighting were just right. But in Lake City there wasn't much art form, except watching the low-lying clouds drop snow in the winter and the fields of wildflowers bloom in the spring.

The Wysockis talked of their love for Lake City, their decision to retreat from the hustle of big cities and suburbia, their delight in the small town and their neighbors, and their dreams for the future. Over dinner Gary and Peter talked about putting together a slide show for the town with our photographs from the walk. Gary would make a sound track. What fun! We all agreed this would be the big event for the end of winter in Lake City.

Between writing the book, trapping, and preparing to leave Lake City in early summer, the slide show took form. Other people in town got involved, Phil Virden and Grant Houston, the editor of the local newspaper, and others. By May the show was ready for a grand premiere.

The marquee read, "Walking Across America, Tonight, 7:30." Word traveled through town as fast as the snow. Gary was more excited than Peter. Tickets were sold at the door, one dollar apiece, and all funds went to the medical center in town. Since there was no hospital, no full-time doctor, and limited medical supplies, everyone had agreed the money should go to the center.

People buzzed with excitement. The little movie theater was packed and more than $140 had been taken in at the door. The theater lights faded, and Gary hit a button on his equipment. Music blasted through the speakers and the photographs came on the screen bigger than life—slides of Peter and Cooper, the mountain man Homer, the black family, scenes from the Appalachians, the Gulf Coast. There were the deserts of Texas, cowboys, photos of us walking, oilmen, animals, sunsets, and more. The music was electrifying, and the audience sat spellbound as if watching a feature movie. There was a standing ovation when it ended. Gary, in his big way, smiled as proud as if he had put on a complete Broadway musical.

It was just too bad that all of Gary's talent was not being used, lying dormant in these stunning mountains that commanded one's attention away from people. Just too bad his gifts were pushed aside in order for him to make a living. He worked as a part time sheriff, a construction worker, storekeeper, and whatever else that would bring in money. Maybe someday Gary could do what he really loved most.

Winter, 1985. Almost seven years had passed since that memorable slide show in Lake City, and Tennessee was having its worst January in history—one snowfall after another and a record seventeen degrees below zero. Peter carried in wood three times a day to keep our Buck Stove pumping out the heat. Our old farmhouse was so large that the wood stove had trouble keeping it warm in the subzero temperatures.

Gary and Jean Wysocki were on their way home to Lake City when they called. They had been to visit her parents in Mississippi to show off their new baby son, Benjamin. We'd not seen each other for several years, and they wanted to see us, our children, and our farm. Could they stop by on their way home, just for one night?

We were thrilled to have them visit and to catch up on all the news. In many ways a part of our heart was still in those mountains, and we hoped to build a cabin someday on three acres we had purchased from Perk Vickers.

When Gary, Jean, daughter Angela, and baby Ben arrived, they were followed by one of the worst snowstorms ever to hit the South. Highways were closed, towns shut down, and travelers' warnings were issued hour after hour. It was much too dangerous for them to leave. The road conditions were so poor that people were being arrested for driving. The Wysockis were stuck with us, snowed in on our Tennessee farm.

Over supper one night we reminisced about the slide show in Lake City. Gary's voice revealed only a faint hint of the excitement he had once felt for the production. He sounded very dull and discouraged and seemed to be at a crossroads in his life.

"We're really praying about what to do," Jean said.

"I'm tired of having to do anything and everything just to pay the bills," Gary sighed.

"And we can't even do that, sometimes," Jean added.

"It's like I'm at a standstill, with no place to go and no future. Now I've got another person to think about." Gary looked down at baby Ben. He was holding him in his giant arms while Jean finished her dinner.

"If you could do anything in the world, anything that you'd really like to do, what would it be?" I asked. My question took them both by surprise. "I mean, laying everything aside, not considering your bills, babies, and mortgage...If you could do anything, what would it be?"

Gary was stumped. He thought and thought. He looked off into the distance, across the open pastures covered in snow. He shook his head, as if to say his wish would be impossible.

"If I could do anything," he mused, "I'd love to get back into some line of stage production like what I did with 'Up with People.' But what a joke. There's nothing like that available. Maybe in Denver, but people with more qualifications already have those jobs. There isn't a demand for people who like to put shows together and manage the stage crew and technical people..."

"It doesn't hurt to dream, to break out of your normal expectations and thoughts," I said, trying to cheer him a little. He reminded me of a big bear who had lost his will to survive.

The next day, late in the afternoon, I reminded Peter to make a phone call on Gary's behalf. Nashville was full of talented people, many artists in every field, and we knew a few of them. It couldn't do any harm. At least we could find out if there was a need for production people. Maybe someone would know someone in Denver and we could make connections for Gary.

When we first met Gary, he was not a Christian. He had become a believer sometime after we walked away from Lake City, and his spiritual growth had been steady although he was not overly zealous. He had prayed about his future for a long time and so had Jean, but they were blocked. Perhaps Gary and Jean were meant to stay put in the mountains they loved.

"Listen, we've got a friend here from Colorado who..." Peter began to tell the story about Gary and Jean. Peter had called a friend of ours, a music writer and producer, who had major best-selling songs to his credit. Maybe our friend would know someone who could help Gary in Colorado.

"I'm glad you called. Would you believe this, we've been praying for just this sort of person to work with us. When can I meet Gary?" the producer said on the other end of the line. Peter about flipped.

Through the ice and snow Peter sped home from his office and ran into the farmhouse. He did several dancing jigs and jumped and clapped his hands together. Gary looked at Peter like he was crazy.

"God's on the move!" Peter shouted. He ran over and slapped Gary on the back and told him to get ready for an interview tomorrow.

Within six weeks, Gary and Jean Wysocki, our faraway mountain friends, had loaded everything they had into a U-Haul, put their cabin up for sale, and come to Tennessee. Gary got the job. God had arranged every detail, had even used the worst winter in Tennessee's history, to have them in the right place at the right time.

But Jesus looked at them and said to them, "With men this is impossible, but with God all things are possible."
Matthew 19:26

14

The Call of the Road

Colorado, 1978. The book was finished, winter was about over, and the call of the road rang in our souls. The people at our publishing house in New York were excited over the manuscript and felt that *A Walk Across America* might be a national best seller. We weren't too concerned because we were headed out, across Engineer Pass, west into Utah, back on the road again. We were now past halfway on our long journey from New Orleans to the Oregon coast.

We waited until late June to leave Lake City because of the glaciers at the high altitudes. We would cross the Rocky Mountains through one of the highest passes in North America where tons of snow were still piled high. About 150 people met in the center of town and walked with us, up Henson Creek, about ten miles to a deserted mining camp called Capitol City. Gary and Jean Wysocki, Perk and Emma Jean Vickers, Jed Vickers, Tom Gross, Tom Ortenburger, Liz Warren, Phil and Carolyn Virden, Tom Baer, Tracey Crutchfield, Bradley and Rusty Hall, Jay Dickman, Irene Brock, and many more came to walk us out of town.

Up and up. With each step we gained altitude and would eventually cross the pass at around thirteen thousand feet. The whole crowd walked until nearly dusk. Perk and Emma Jean had organized a big cookout for us and arrived with a carload of food. While Perk cooked the steaks over an open fire, huge amounts of beans, salad, bread, sodas, and champagne were spread out. The air was so clean I savored each breath. The mountains were green with vegetation. White waterfalls tumbled off cliffs in every direction, and the food was so rich with flavor at this altitude I felt on top of the world. Even Perk's cigar smelled wonderful to me. The laughter of all our friends echoed through the hills and filled the grassy valley where we were. It was a great mountain party.

In the quietness of our tent the first night, camped in the splendor of the high Rockies, I wrote a prayer in my diary: "Go with us, Lord, as we begin the walk westward. Withdraw not Your Spirit from us, but lead us, favor us, and cause us to bring fruit for Thy Kingdom. Lead us not into temptation but deliver us from evil. In Jesus' name we pray."

My prayer came none too soon. The next day, after our friends had returned to Lake City, we were crossing the highest peak, snowwalking on ten-foot drifts beside sheer dropoffs. Somehow I lost my footing, fell, and began to slide. The glacier was like a giant playground slide. Slick. Steep. Fast. Down...down I slid. Peter screamed at me through the howling wind to dig my pack into the snow, but I didn't hear him. I was on my back, my legs jerking, trying to stop. I had to stop soon or I would fly over the sharp cliff and fall to my death in the gully below.

I clawed at the snow, but it was crusty and I found nothing to grab. There was no time to scream. I kept sliding. Suddenly, I jerked and slowed. My backpack had lodged itself into a small crevice and my run-away body had stopped.

It was nothing I had done. I didn't know why I had stopped. I was still flat on my back with my heels stuck into a ridge of snow. Slowly, carefully, not wanting to dislodge my-self and start another horrible slide, I raised my head and looked. I was right at the edge of the cliff, less than three feet from death. I was stunned, afraid to move. Carefully, I rolled over and braced myself. I started to shake. I looked up at Pe-ter standing high above, his arms outstretched, waiting to help me up. Slowly, cautiously, and tearfully I crawled up-ward until I reached him.

Down...down...down we climbed, from the great San Juan Mountains, on twisting trails that still were treach-erous. We passed through Ouray, Montrose, Delta and neared Grand Junction. We had come from one extreme to another. From the high peaks and cold, blistering winds at the top of Engineer Pass to the flat, arid desert of western Colorado where it was ninety-nine degrees in the shade. We were within two days of reaching Utah where water could be found only every fifty to one hundred miles. We had a seri-ous problem. There was no way to cross Utah in July without water.

We happened to be in Grand Junction on a Sunday and for the first time since we had left New Orleans two years earlier we decided to ask for help. We had to find some-one who would be willing to bring us water while we crossed Utah, but who? Where would we begin to find such a per-son? We were walking through town, looking for a place to rest, when we passed a church—the First Assembly of God. Something about this place drew us. The first phone booth we came to, Peter looked in the yellow pages and found the church's number. He called, and Pastor Cope answered.

"Sir, I know this will sound crazy, but my wife and I are walking across America and we will be entering Utah to-morrow. We were wondering if there would be someone you know who could bring water to us?" Peter said.

There was a long...long pause on the other end of the line. Peter's request must have sounded strange. Preachers get phone calls all the time from people asking for food, money, and a place to stay; but water to help two backpackers cross Utah was a little out of the ordinary. Peter quickly tried to explain who we were, what we were doing, and that we were Christians.

Peter listened while the pastor spoke.

"Yeah, I guess we could, " Peter said hesitantly. "But all we have to wear are our shorts and walking clothes." The preacher had asked us to attend his church that evening and give our testimony. Maybe someone would volunteer to help us.

A few hours later we were sitting in the back row of a church full of people, dressed in our walking clothes, when Pastor Cope asked us to come forward. Everyone stared. We walked forward as reverently as we could, conscious of how out of place we looked among these people dressed in their Sunday best. We tried to walk softly in our heavy boots. I had combed my curly hair and put on a little lipstick. Peter had dampened a paper towel and washed his face. We looked as though we had just dropped in from the wilds of the range, which of course we had. Our eyes squinted in the bright spotlights as we faced the congregation. Pastor Cope introduced us. He had read Peter's article in *National Geographic*.

"We really appreciate your pastor's letting us come here tonight," Peter said. "My wife and I are walking across America, headed across Utah, and we were hoping someone here would feel led by the Lord to help us, to bring us water across the desert." Peter cleared his throat, obviously nervous. "And, by the way, I apologize for the way we look. But when you're walking across the country, you can't carry a suit and tie."

People laughed. The tension eased and several hands sprung up. The pastor asked those people to talk to him after the service and arrangements would be worked out to bring us water in Utah.

Ron Maupin became our water courier. After the service, he and his wife, Kitty, invited us to their house trailer. "We hope to buy a home on the ground soon," Ron laughed. He was a former rodeo performer and showed us pictures of himself riding a bull. Ron was about thirty with carrot-red hair and a complexion to match. He worked on a construction crew but knew he would have some slack time during the next couple of weeks and could bring us water.

I had thought Texas was hot, but Utah was hotter. We were on Interstate 70, our faces pointed straight west into the boiling sun. We carried a little thermometer which we set on the pavement. The dial read 132 degrees. A sign along the highway said, "Next Food and Water, 107 miles." If I had not already walked all the way from New Orleans, I would have fainted reading that sign.

In the middle of the dry desert, gnats and flies surrounded us and formed a constant cloud. It was impossible to talk without having gnats fly into our mouths and it was too hot to keep swatting them. I finally realized that they were thirsty, too, and were looking for moisture. Our beads of sweat were just what they wanted.

In order to keep the flying pests out of my eyes and nose, I pulled a bushy weed out of the ground and stuck it into the brim of my hat. The weed hung down over my face and whenever the flies and gnats buzzed too close I threw my head back and forth to chase them away. With our bulging blue backpacks, our golfing umbrellas attached overhead, and a bush hanging in my face, no wonder car horns honked and we were the talk of every C.B. along the interstate.

The great Salt Lake Valley lay before us, dotted with orchards and communities that throbbed with an energy we had not seen since Dallas. When Brigham Young had crossed the Wasatch Mountains in July, 1847, and looked across the fertile bowl, he said, "This is the place." I could see why he was so enthused. What a contrast the valley was to the bar-

ren desert that surrounded it. Most of the green trees and orchards hugged the snow-capped mountain range and drank
from the melting snow. The sight was beautiful, soothing to
our eyes.

But the geography of the area was not the only thing
that seemed different. The people in the stores, on the streets,
and in the neighborhoods looked different, too—normal but
at the same time unusual. They had a clean and healthy look
to them. Wholesome and preoccupied. We began to notice
little things as we walked through Provo, Midvale, and on
into Salt Lake City.

In every café there was no public smoking. We really
liked that and had never seen it before. In one restaurant a
sign read, "Smoking men and women are like wormy apples,
they drop before their time." It felt good to see people so
health-conscious, and it showed on their faces. Most of the
women had lovely, clear complexions, and everyone had glis-
tening white teeth. Before long we noticed that most young
couples had three, four, five, even six children, all of them
fair, mostly blond and blue-eyed. We had never seen so many
pregnant women.

The streets of Salt Lake City were lined with colorful
flowers, neat lawns, and clean sidewalks and parking lots.
People bustled, always in motion, working, working. There
was an industrious spirit in the air. Nothing was idle or still
except the graveyards we passed. Suddenly I noticed there
were no crosses anywhere on the graves, unlike New Orleans
where every tombstone had a big crucifix or statue of Jesus.
Then I looked up at the steeple on one of the churches. The
lettering on the outside of the building said, The Church of
Jesus Christ of Latter-Day Saints (The Mormons), but there
was no cross. That seemed odd.

We felt a pull to the center of the city, to the sacred
Mormon temple. We had heard that all Mormons hope to go
there sometime, to attend one of the services. We stopped in
a grocery store on the way to buy cold drinks. The woman

behind the counter was brooding over our lounging around in her store, so we tried to be friendly. We asked her directions, typical tourist questions about the area, and then we hit the jackpot—"How far is it to the temple?"

She loosened up and began to talk. She had been a Mormon all her life. It was her dream to worship in the Mormon Tabernacle, but she didn't have the special card required to get in. She handed us a pamphlet to read so we would understand her religion and hopefully accept it. With strong emotion she told us that the Church of Jesus Christ of Latter-Day Saints was the "restored" church, the true church here on earth.

I took the literature and thanked her. I acted interested and told her I had been a student of the Bible for a long time and had even gone to seminary. She politely told me the Bible could not be relied on unless it was "properly translated." And that could only have been done by the founder of the Mormon religion, Joseph Smith.

I was beginning to feel a little guarded, but she proceeded to tell us the whole story of her faith. It had all started in 1820 when Joseph Smith was fifteen years old. He had gone into a grove of trees south of Palmyra, New York, to ask God which church or sect he should join. He had a vision. Two personages stood above him in the air. And one of them said he should not join any church but should follow the fullness of the gospel which would be made known to him in the future.

"What happened? I've never heard of this before," I asked out of curiosity.

She was glad to keep going. Her sincere eyes were fixed on me. She said that about three years later a heavenly being appeared to Joseph, an angel who called himself Moroni. The angel said he had buried some gold plates, engraved in an ancient language, and Joseph was chosen to translate them, to restore the gospel to the church. He had to wear special spectacles to translate the golden plates and the book that came out of this was called *The Book of Mormon*. The book was written in 1829 and on April 6, 1830, The Church of Jesus Christ of Latter-Day Saints was formally organized. Joseph Smith had received a new revelation making Saint John's Revelation in the New Testament obsolete.

I was speechless. She was leaning over the counter, really warmed up now, and must have thought my silence meant that I wanted to hear more.

"Another person who can translate the Bible correctly is our church president who has a direct link back to Joseph and to God," she said. She told me that he was a prophet, and whatever he heard from God was infallible. *The Book of Mormon, Doctrine and Covenants, Pearl of Great Price* and all the writings of Joseph Smith were the complete inspired word of God. "Not the Bible," she said matter-of-factly.

I asked the woman about the national news coverage the Mormon church had received the past month. The church president had announced that blacks could become priests and newspapers had carried the controversial story, "Mormons Get New Revelation, Blacks Accepted." For more than 148 years, the Mormon church had banished blacks because according to one of their doctrines, "Cain was cursed with a dark skin, he became the father of negroes and those spirits who are not worthy to receive the priesthood are born through his lineage."

Although people across the country were puzzled by the Mormons' new policy, which seemed to be a result of public pressure rather than a new revelation, this woman found no reason to be unsettled. "The church president is a prophet and he's heard from God and there's no error," she concluded.

She gave me a stack of leaflets. "Look at the facts," she said. "Mormons are the fastest growing religion in the world, and they have a strong moral code against drugs, homosexuality, abortion, premarital sex, and marital infidelity. Nothing keeps Mormons from being with their children every

Monday night. Mormons have lower cancer and heart disease rates and are known for their outstanding hard work and honesty. They are the most committed people to their families and church anywhere."

The clerk paused, half expecting me to join her religion on the spot. Where was Peter? He had slipped around the aisle and was reading a magazine, leaving me alone to hear her out. What she was saying sounded convincing, but what about those churches with no crosses?

"Mormons have famous people among their ranks like the Osmonds and George Romney who was a top Republican candidate for president and a secretary of HUD. The Mormon Tabernacle Choir has been heard on the radio for more than fifty years," she continued. "The Mormons have more than thirty thousand missionaries around the world, and they have some of the most advanced technology anywhere. They have seminaries, schools, universities, and they recruit students from every state and country. The Mormons' Relief Society is one of the largest women's groups in the world."

In the valley protected by the Wasatch Mountains, Mormonism was a pervasive fact. Everybody was either a Mormon or going to become one. I had heard that the religion was a mighty force in Utah and throughout the West and was spreading as fast as range fire. How could anyone stand against it? How could anyone not believe?

When I tried to bring the conversation back to the Bible, I could see we were worlds apart. She did not want to talk about the Bible. All the Mormons' fantastic works and industries and well-known personalities outshone the fact that my faith was built on the teachings in the Bible. The Bible alone. Nothing added. I had a deep inner resistance to their angel Moroni, now depicted in a golden statue on top of their temple. I knew no such angel was mentioned in either the Old or New Testament of the Bible.

Stories about angels I'd learned in Sunday school as a child flashed through my mind. Paul's letter to the Galatians read, "But even if we, or *an angel from heaven*, preach any other gospel to you than what we have preached to you, let him be accursed. As we have said before, so now I say again, if anybody preaches any other gospel to you than what you have received, let him be accursed."

Of course this wouldn't matter to the clerk because she didn't accept the validity of the Bible. In fact, according to these leaflets, there were lots of things Mormons believed that were not in the Bible, such as Jesus was born of a fleshly union, Jesus was married to Mary and Martha, Jesus would come again to the promised land of Salt Lake City, salvation could only be gained through good works, and women could not be saved apart from men. Mormons also believed, contrary to the Bible, that there would be marriages and child-bearing in the next world, that the more children a man had, the more honor and glory he would have in eternity, that God the Father was flesh and bones, and that there could be no salvation outside the Mormon church. They also thought spirits lived with God and were waiting for bodies to inhabit. So, Mormon men had to produce lots of children, fleshly bodies, so the spirits could have a resting place.

The more I heard, the more I could see how complex and tangled were Mormon beliefs. The religion was a giant puzzle, with pieces from the Bible, pieces from Joseph Smith, and a hundred years of more pieces from their doctrinal changes. It was too overwhelming for me.

We finally left the grocery store. It felt good to walk away from the woman and her piles of information about how to get to heaven. The Mormon Way. It was a lot different from the uncluttered gospel of the Bible. As we walked out of her life, away from Salt Lake City and its religious devotees, I pulled out my tiny New Testament and looked up 2 Corinthians 11:3-4.

But I fear, lest somehow, as the serpent deceived Eve by his craftiness. So your minds may be corrupted from the simplicity that is in Christ.

For if he who comes preaches another Jesus whom we have not preached, or if you receive a different spirit which you have not received, or a different gospel which you have not accepted, you may well put up with it.

Nothing could budge me from believing what the verses said about the simplicity of faith in Christ. Simple...understandable...clear... That's what I liked about the Jesus Christ I followed and served.

Would that all 1st time christians would think, feel + follow Christ so humbly.

15

Jedidiah

We left Salt Lake City in September 1978 bearing a strong feeling we had to reach the Pacific Northwest by fall or early winter. Peter had been on the road five years, and it had been more than two years for me. The time had come to finish our walk. We both sensed this and realized only Idaho and Oregon were left to cross.

On an overcast and stormy day we passed through Kaysville and Ogden, Utah. An earthy fragrance of freshly cut hay and grass was in the air, and farmers were busy harvesting everything from peaches to corn. We wondered how the great agricultural valley would withstand all the new growth and industry moving in from the East. The farmland was slowly being devoured by more houses and businesses. And if urban sprawl didn't take over, an earthquake might. We found out that the largest earthquake fault in the world was right there, along the Wasatch Mountains.

As we walked through the busy streets and sidewalks breathing fumes of heavy traffic, we passed a statue. The sculpture was of a pioneer trapper from the 1820s, long before Brigham Young arrived with his new religion. The memorial sign read, "Jedidiah Strong Smith, Minister to mountain men with a Bible in one hand and a rifle in the other." The figure was impressive, with strong looks and a heroic bearing.

Suddenly it hit me: if we ever had a son, Jedidiah would be his name! Hopefully, he'd be strong in character like this man and just as God-fearing. We already liked the name "Jed" because of a young friend back in Lake City named Jed Vickers, who was a nephew to Perk. Now we were certain. This was the second time the name had stood out to us and it felt right. Jedidiah. We would call our son Jedidiah. Jed for short. That name had *umph!* Later we learned it meant "beloved of the Lord" and was used in reference to King Solomon in the Bible.

If we ever had a son... The past few months I had been secretly yearning for a child, especially since I'd just had my thirtieth birthday. My situation seemed upside-down. Most of my friends were married, already had two or three kids and their first home, and were on their way to becoming established. And here I was, my house strapped on my back, walking fifteen miles a day, never knowing where my next meal would come from, and getting older by the mile.

These thoughts gnawed inside me, but this was no time to talk about having a baby. Doctors said it might take a year to get pregnant after I quit using the birth-control pills. So Peter and I decided I should stop taking them.

Maybe, if we were lucky, I would get pregnant sometime after we ended the walk and after the book had come out. Or, maybe never. When doubts about having children would creep into my mind, I would have a mental war and tell all my fears to go away. Walking across America was exactly what God wanted me to do, and He would surely bless me for obeying. Being thirty years old was no problem for God. Had my memory failed me? Had not God blessed Sarah with a child long after she passed thirty, long after she passed the change of life? Why should I compare myself to what society said was the normal age to have children, the average thing to do? But I didn't want to be another Sarah, who must have used a walking cane to keep up with her baby Isaac. Stop it! If Sarah had not been able to bear and care for a child in her old age, God would not have permitted her to have one. Oh, wasn't the name Jedidiah fabulous? I dreamed of that day.

Winter, 1982. We were preparing to go to the Sunday night Christmas play and party at our little church in town. The Lord had answered my prayers for children; our darling Rebekah, born after the end of the walk across America, was for the first time about to see and understand the shepherds, the wise men, and Joseph and Mary holding baby Jesus. She was now three, and Christmas was taking on special meaning—the true meaning. And she understood we were about to have another baby, too. Brownies were in the oven and everything was almost ready for us to leave for church when it happened.

"Pack your bags and plan to stay in the hospital," Dr. Sam Kuykendall told me over the phone.

"But I'm not ready. I have brownies in the oven and can't we go to the Christmas play first?" I asked. I felt no pain and was not in labor, but my water had broken. Since our first child had been born by Caesarean, it was too risky for me to go into labor.

"I'll meet you at the hospital in thirty minutes," the doctor said.

In our small-town hospital, Peter wasn't allowed in the operating room, so my dear friend Brenda Hebert, who was a nurse, stood over me during the surgery, rubbing my temples, talking to me, and telling me to take deep breaths. I was awake throughout the delivery. At 9:52 on that Sunday night, December 19, the doctor grinned and said, "It's a boy." We named him Jedidiah Gorton Jenkins and he was beautiful. Our darling son was here. So long prayed for, so long dreamed about. How could God be so good to us?

As I lay in my hospital bed on that cold winter's night, only three days before Christmas, I remembered that statue in Utah and cried tears of thankfulness. There was so much to be grateful for. We had finally bought a farm and an old house we planned to restore; our second book, *The Walk West*, was a bestseller and publishers wanted more books. We were planning a trip to Alaska with my parents; we had started a new business; and our old friends from the Baptist seminary, Wally and Brenda Hebert, now lived near us. We had joined the First Baptist Church and had lots of new friends and neighbors in our little farming community, and most of all, we had a precious little girl. Now, a son.

In my diary I jotted down how I felt: "Rebekah and Jed are truly gifts from God, and my soul is full and my dreams fulfilled. My cup runs over and I feel satisfied. The cry of my heart is that Peter and I be godly parents, that we train our children in the ways of the Lord, and that they choose to walk with God all the days of their lives and choose Christian mates."

I never dreamed of what was about to happen.

A few weeks later I was inside another hospital room, crying more tears, but this time anxious and fearful ones for our baby Jed. He was barely two months old as he lay strapped to a cold hospital bed with tubes stuck in his arms and nose. We were in a semiprivate room at Vanderbilt Hospital in Nashville, one of the best pediatric hospitals in the country. Jed looked full-faced, pink, and sweet as he rested on the big bed. He was so loved and wanted, just the opposite of the tiny baby girl in the bed next to him.

She was the frailest baby I'd ever seen. Her black skin looked even darker against the sterile white sheets.

"Her mama won't come see her. This is her seventh child, just left it here," the nurse said with a frown. She shook her head in disgust. "Her mama is only twenty-two years old."

The baby girl was five months old but weighed less than ten pounds. Jed was twice her size. She cried a different cry from any I'd ever heard. It was a wounded sound, shrill, and almost like the meow of a cat. Not a normal cry, not a cry of hunger or a plea for a dry diaper, but rather a piercing and tormenting cry that haunted me as I listened to it. My baby boy lay plump and quiet as he waited for surgery. The tiny infant girl cried on.

Dawn broke in gray clouds and a soft drizzle of rain. Peter had stayed until after midnight and would be back in the morning. I had been awake all night, sitting beside Jed's bed, watching fresh blood drip into his veins, preparing him for his 8:00 A.M. operation. He had cried himself to sleep from hunger because he was not allowed nourishment before the operation. Every now and then he would whimper. My heart hurt. Morning had come and there was no more time for prayers. The surgeons were waiting and they came for my son.

Not long after they rolled Jed out of my sight, the infant girl in the next bed woke up and began to howl. "Eh-ow, eh-ow," she cried. Her little body flopped up and down on the bed like a fish out of water. She slapped her tightened body so violently against the mattress and bed rails that the nurses had to tie her down. People walked by the open door and looked in at the strange baby, but no one wanted to touch her, comfort her or hold her. The nurses were too busy. Every time the baby girl squealed, a two-inch hernia inflated and popped out from her navel like a balloon. I had never seen such a repulsive thing.

I could bear it no longer. Between Jedidiah who was being cut open at that moment and this abandoned infant, I thought my heart would explode from the ache. A sense of motherhood overwhelmed me. I didn't care what the nurses said. I unstrapped the black baby, jerking and gnarled as she was, and held her as tight as I could against my chest. In my softest voice I whispered to the baby, trying to soothe and calm her. It saddened me to think there were no special arms waiting to hold this child, no one to care for and nurture her.

Up and down the halls I walked, avoiding the curious stares from the nurses. No matter how I tried to comfort her, she wouldn't stop wailing. Her wounds were so deep my temporary arms could not erase the damage. The tiny person already knew the world had given her a cruel blow. It was so pitiful I wondered if I could bear up under all the pain that surrounded me. Finally, she went to sleep. I laid her down gently on the steel-framed bed.

With my knees drawn under my chin I sat on the window ledge in the hospital room, waiting, staring at the February rain turning to snow. People were scurrying outside in every direction. Some were hurrying to work, others to school. Many were off to run their businesses and others were dodging traffic. I wondered if any of those people knew how I felt? Only another parent who has endured a long night watching a sick child seesaw back and forth between danger and safety knows the moments of unflinching faith— and of dark despair. The anguish. The fear of losing a child. The hours of soul-searching and prayer. Finally, the final acceptance that what will be, will be.

There came a knock on the door. Before I could wipe the smeared mascara off my face, there stood Homer. A smile covered his fifty-five-year-old face. His oversized eyes shone through the thick eyeglasses he wore, and his gray hair matched the gray suit he wore most every Sunday.

Homer Kelley. The country preacher who'd grown up in a holler back in the hills of Tennessee and had made moonshine when he was a boy. He was a hell raiser back then, but for the last twenty-five years he'd been a heaven raiser. This was the man who shouted out faith on Sundays, who cried when people "got saved," and who told his congregation with a broken voice, "If there's anybody here who needs me, anytime, day or night, I'll crawl to get to you if I have to." My pastor had come.

Peter arrived from the farm a short time later and for the next hour and a half, Homer told us one funny story after another of his boyhood days, what it was like growing up dirt-poor during the depression, and how he could only see out of one eye and hear out of one ear. Peter and I realized what a sacrifice it was for him to be with us thirty-five miles from home to sit with us through the surgery.

"Tell me, Homer, if you can only see out of one eye, then how do you drive? And all the way here to Nashville?" Peter asked.

"Just get in the far right lane and stay put," Homer said.

At 9:55 A.M. Dr. Skip Neblett found us at the snack bar sitting around a table. Jedidiah had come through the surgery just fine and all was well. Homer, Peter, and I joined hands and thanked God for his goodness to us. We were relieved; such a weight had been lifted off our shoulders. Only then, after the surgeon had given us the good news, did Homer tell us the rest of his story. Many years ago he and his wife, Dolly, had been thrilled to have a baby girl. When she was just two months old, the same age as Jedidiah, she had become ill. Until that moment, Homer had never told us his baby girl died.

These things I have spoken to you, that in Me you may have peace. In the world you will have tribulation; but be of good cheer, I have overcome the world.

John 16:33

We then that are strong ought to bear the infirmities of the weak, and not to please ourselves.

Romans 15:1 KJV

16

On the Right Side of the Tracks

I n the fall of 1978 we were still in Utah, headed northwest toward Idaho. Today was like most other days on the walk—slow, one step after another, one mile after another— yet it was different. We were walking along a set of railroad tracks near the spot where the historic rail had been fastened together in 1869 with a golden spike, uniting the east and the west, making coast to coast travel by train possible for the first time.

The tracks were so polished, like shiny silver, we could tell they were used every day. We kept looking back to make sure a fast Amtrack didn't slip up on us. Not many days earlier we'd been walking on a curve in a set of tracks when a quiet, speeding, Amtrack came upon us. We had not heard the train and literally had to jump off the tracks into a deep gully to keep from being hit.

When we walked on railroad tracks I often thought about the legend I learned as a child; if you walk nine rails without falling off, you will find a lock of hair from your future husband or wife under the last joint. It was a silly legend, but it brought back many memories of my childhood. I could remember the years I walked home from school, skipping from one creosote-blackened railroad tie to another, kicking rocks and looking for anything unusual. As a kid I tried to walk the nine rails, held together by heavy iron joints and nailed down to the ties with steel spikes, but fell off every time because they were so narrow. One time I had found a dime.

How could I have known, at the tender age of ten, that walking those narrow rails was a harbinger of things to come, eighteen years in the future? In my innocent childhood I never dreamed that one day I would walk hundreds of miles on railroad tracks, crossing the country with my husband beside me...

I remember one winter day hurrying home from school so I could skate on the ice pond and play with Smokey, our dog, and with my twelve-year-old brother, Jimmy, and my six-year-old sister, Vicky. I could hear them laughing across the tracks. They were already on the pond having a good time. I walked as fast as I could. We would have only an hour before dark and supper time, and I had to take my books into the house and change clothes. My feet were aching from the cold because my socks were stuck in my coat pocket. I had worn my best flats to school, but since I didn't like the way they looked with socks, I had taken them off after leaving the house that morning.

Snow was starting to spit from gray clouds. The Frisco train blasted its air horn twice, and I could hear it rattling down the tracks. I would easily get across before it reached me, but there were lots of other cars I had to get around before I reached home—wooden box cars, steel hopper cars loaded with coal, and flat-bed cars waiting to be filled. They stretched as far as I could see either way, lined up for more than a mile. I didn't feel very ladylike crawling under the cars or hopping the couplers between them, but what else could I do? Jimmy and Vicky were playing on the ice pond, and their laughter could be heard for a long way. I could hear the sounds of other kids who were there, too.

I squatted, then crawled under a Sante Fe boxcar away from the steel wheels that were still rocking and screeching to a stop. I was careful not to get dirty. Gobs of grease were everywhere. Air brakes let off loud hissing sounds, and then a diesel locomotive revved up its motor. I moved fast and hoped the switchman wouldn't catch me. No sooner had I reached the other side of all the trains than the last row of boxcars jerked and banged into each other all the way down the line. That was close! I was in too big a hurry to care.

The winter sun was about to set, and I could see home. Our big yard with apple, pear, cherry, and walnut trees was covered with an inch of snow. Out back was a shed we called the smokehouse, where we played hide and seek. I ran as fast as I could up the hill, hopped across the ditch, flew past the outdoor toilet, down the fence beside the garden spot, and arrived, breathless, at the back screen door.

Our white frame house stood out against the darkening sky. It was an older four-room building with no indoor plumbing. We had to bathe in a number two galvanized tub on the back porch. During one such bath, when the water was already a milky color from the Ivory soap, my brother and a neighbor boy, Mike Ross, came in the back door and walked right by me. I screamed, threatened them, and wanted to kill them both for embarrassing me. They just snickered, pointed their fingers at me, and walked as slowly as they could across the porch out into the yard.

Since then the old back porch had been enclosed and made into a kitchen. Mother had done most of the carpentry work herself. But our house still did not have insulation, and the linoleum floors were always cold. Mother would hang curtains over the bedroom doors to keep the heat from the one gas stove from leaving the center of the house.

As simple as our house was, our neighbors' houses made ours look modern. Not only did the blacktop end in front of our house, and we lived at the edge of town on the wrong side of the tracks, but we lived in one of the poorest neighborhoods in town. None of our neighbors could read or write. Most of them were country farmers who had come to town to live. Many of them came to my mother for help answering their mail, filling out their taxes, and paying their bills. She never refused them and often drove them to the store.

Mother had time for the strays, the hoboes, too. They would hop off the trains and stand at our back door, asking for food. Sometimes they stole our clothes off the line if they needed them. Mother kept leftover cornbread and beans for such as these and never sent anyone away hungry.

In the distance some coon dogs were barking. They were over on the pond with Jimmy and Vicky.

"I'm home," I yelled, slamming the back door. It was covered with plastic to keep out rain and cold wind.

Mother popped out from behind a curtain that hung between the kitchen and the storage/wash room. Her short, red hair was in bobby pins, curled in tight little circles all over her head. "Barbara, why did you take off your socks on the way to school this morning?" I was caught off guard. How did she know that? Who had told her? Had she seen me stop on the way to school and take off my socks? "Don't you have sense enough to know you'll catch pneumonia?"

At the worst possible moment I sneezed! I could never get away with anything, it seemed. I always got caught, and if I had done something really bad, I would get a lot more than a scolding. I never suspected that my brother had told on me. Jimmy wasn't a tattletale, but he would try anything to get rid of me and keep me from tagging along behind him. I was always at his heels wanting to go fishing, to track rabbits, to play ball, but in his eyes I was just a dumb girl. He especially tried to ditch me when his boyfriends were around, like now, skating on the pond.

"Can I go skate on the pond?"

"Get the clothes off the line, then you can," Mother said.

My fingers turned red and stiff as I pinched the wooden clothespins and pulled the stiff, icy sheets off the line. The cold air burned my lungs. I was hurrying so fast and taking such deep breaths that my chest hurt. Why didn't we have a clothes dryer like other people? I was embarrassed because we were so poor—we didn't even have an automatic washing machine. Instead, Mother used an old wringer-type washer with two galvanized rinse tubs that took up the whole kitchen, which was not very big to begin with. It took her a whole day to do the wash.

Hurriedly, I ran the armload of sheets into the house, my face nearly hidden inside them. They smelled like the outside air—fresh, cold, and pure. Mother stood behind the ironing board, her face lightly flushed, pushing the iron back and forth across a cotton shirt. "I'm walking the floor over you," blared Ernest Tubb from the radio that sat on the window ledge. I could smell a pot of vegetable soup cooking on the stove and knew what we would be having for supper: hot soup and cornbread. My mouth watered, but I had to make tracks, fast, in order to skate on the pond.

"Get home before dark," Mother said as I ran out. "Yer Daddy will be home soon for supper."

My daddy, Ernie Pennell, never said much. I didn't know if he was just a quiet man or too tired to talk after working ten to twelve hours a day. He owned and operated a Mobil truck stop about eight miles south of our town, Poplar Bluff, Missouri, and spent most of his time pumping gas, repairing engines, changing tires, washing windshields, and talking to truck drivers in the café next door. He drank about a dozen cups of coffee each day, trying to be sociable with his customers.

I thought him to be most handsome, with fair pink skin and jet black hair. According to Mother many of the girls near Purman, Missouri, had dreamed of catching Ernie Pennell when he was young. He had grown up on a farm in Ripley County and attended the small one-room "Cyclone School."

Daddy was smart but there hadn't been much time for schooling when he was a boy. Crops had to be planted and harvested, and he peddled strawberries with his dad. Daddy only went through the eighth grade, but he had a natural knack for fixing machines and became an expert mechanic. While we were small children he bought a gas station and garage and called it "Ernie's Motorway," which was so successful that people would come from miles around to have their cars fixed. The only problem was the long hours, at least ten a day, seven days a week. Not much time was left for Mother or us kids.

When Daddy walked into the house after work he always asked two questions: "What's for supper?" and "Any mail?" He said little the rest of the evening. His thick, calloused hands were as black as his hair, smudged with grit and grease. His gray-green uniform had a patch over the shirt pocket that said, "Ernie," and he smelled of gasoline and oil.

Mother, the former Betty Jo Crain, wasn't quiet! She was feisty, strong-willed, and determined, and she stayed in constant motion, always operating in high gear.

"Set the table, get the cornbread out of the oven, fill Daddy's glass with ice water," Mother would say in one breath.

Mother was fiery, her temper as hot as her beautiful red hair. She was quick on the draw about everything she said and did and was short on patience. But her heart would melt easily, and she always meant to do what was right. In her youth she had been a stunning beauty, her wavy red hair falling beyond her shoulders in long tongues of fire. Her features were delicate, and her teeth were as white as fine china.

Sparks flew when eyes were laid on Betty Jo, born to Walter and Annie Crain. She was a mighty fine filly.

Although they were quite different, Mother and Daddy were a good match for each other and tried to raise us without a lot of open arguments or conflict. In those days it was not proper for families to talk about their problems, to seek any kind of counseling, or to let anyone outside the house know there were troubles. And, like every other normal family, we had our share of them. Daddy worked too hard and too long, while Mother was left to take care of three kids. In the late 1950s and early 1960s fathers weren't expected to be "involved," to share the workload in the home, to cross the role boundaries, or to encourage open communication.

Because of the stress from these circumstances, all of us felt a frustration, but we didn't know what to do about it. We each found a way to cope and hang together as a family. Mother stayed busy with her sewing, gardening, canning, art work, and running the home. She held her family and home in first place, never being a busybody or gadabout. Daddy worked, sacrificing himself so that we had a roof, enough clothing, and plenty of food. Vicky became a tomboy, preferring dogs and horses and climbing trees to wearing dresses, primping, and looking pretty. Jimmy played with the dogs, fished, and stayed on the creek bank as much as possible. And, in the midst of these uncomplicated but hard times, I learned to cope by "getting saved."

My girlfriend from grade school, Martha Jeffries, had invited me to go with her and her parents to a revival. I had never been to a revival, although we children attended Sunday school at a little church up the road. Each Sunday morning Mother faithfully dressed us and sent us off to church. She and Daddy didn't go to church because Daddy worked every Sunday and she wouldn't go without him.

On November 11, 1960, I went with Martha and her

parents to the Black River Baptist Church, a little one-room building many miles back into the country. The preacher talked about Jesus and the Holy Spirit in a way I had never heard before. He brought down heaven. I went to the altar and fell to my knees, weeping for reasons I couldn't understand. I accepted Jesus Christ as my savior. An old woman with a big bosom held me in her arms and spoke to me kindly while I cried. Afterward I felt as free as a bird on the first day of flight, light as a feather, as clean as if I had been washed in pure spring water.

My conversion was very emotional. Something strong had happened to me, and my interests were immediately changed. I became concerned about spiritual things, attending church, and reading my Bible. I had a new seriousness about myself, a passion for God that would make some people think I was a fanatic. Within a short time I joined the South Poplar Bluff General Baptist Church. Later, I became a youth leader, taught Sunday school, was the church secretary, went on religious retreats, and even attended a Christian college. My pastor, Curtis Eaker, and his wife LaVerne, took me under their wing, like one of their own children, and guided me through my teenage years.

After my conversion I was baptized the old-time way by Reverend Eaker in the Black River, which had never felt so cold or so good. I came up out of that river holding on to the preacher and to God with a grip that would never let go. Years would pass, and at times I would try to hide from God while doing the wild things that college kids do, acting like someone I wasn't. But God had a hold on me and would never let me go. Whenever I would party too long, drink too much, or pretend it was all right to live as I pleased, God would haunt me and be at my coattails wherever I went. Those were fun-filled, yet miserable days. I learned that there was pleasure in sin, but only for a season, and that I could never get away from God. He owned me. He had a purpose for my life.

"Barb-bree-e-e-e-e." My granddad hollered across the yard that separated our house from his.

I was sure that he had seen Jimmy and me. That meant trouble. We had "rolled our own" and had been smoking rabbit grass and old grapevines behind the shed. Vicky had threatened to tattle on us, and I bet she had done so because she was nowhere in sight. Boy, would I get her later!

"Micky-e-e-e-e-e-e." Granddad hollered again. He was nearly eighty years old and never did get our names right. He called me "Barbree" and Vicky "Micky." We always giggled behind his back because he was so hard of hearing.

"Yer Granny wants you," Granddad said.

Granny and Granddad, my mother's parents, lived next door to us most of my childhood. Walter and Annie Crain were the greatest possession we had on South Eleventh Street. They were always there next door, in their tiny, old house, which was just a shack, badly leaning to one side. After more than fifty years of marriage, it was all they had to show for their labor. Yet, neither of them seemed to mind. They were satisfied with what material things they had, satisfied with good food to eat, wood to keep the fires going in their potbelly stove, fresh air, and sunshine. They seemed always grateful for a day with no aches or pains, a day to plow in the garden or pick a fresh rose or quarrel at the chickens for not laying more eggs. Their greatest luxury was a portable black and white television set and getting to watch "Rawhide" and "Gunsmoke" on Friday and Saturday nights.

I usually spent Friday nights with them and would sleep with Granny in her giant featherbed, buried under several of her homemade quilts. She snored, and many times I would have to shake her and tell her that she was keeping me awake. She would grin and pinch me with her toes under the covers, then go back to snoring.

Granddad hollered again, "Barb-bre-e-e-e-e-e." He stood like a statue, motionless. Watching me running toward him, his blue eyes seemed to peer into the soul. I ran by him,

slamming the backdoor, kicking the mud off my shoes.
Granny had been cooking supper and pulled a berry cobbler
out of the oven on the wood stove. She knew that was my favorite. I would be spending the night with them. Granddad
didn't ask me what I had been doing out back with Jimmy. I
breathed a sigh of relief. I told them that tonight Jimmy was
going to the picture show and Vicky would stay home and
play with the dog.

"What was you youngin's doin' out back?" Granny
asked. She was bending over the table and couldn't see my
face.

"Nothin much, just playin'."

"Wash up and let's give thanks," Granny said.

Eating supper with Granny and Granddad was always
the same. In fact, everything about them stayed the same,
giving us kids a feeling that life was stable and not to be
feared. Everyone would live to be old and would probably
get a little cranky with arthritis or have to wear reading
glasses or drink prune juice to keep bodily functions regular.

Granddad drank black coffee the way he did at every
meal, coffee that had boiled on the stove all day and turned
dirt black and thick. He dipped his bread in gravy or grease,
whichever was on the table. My old Granny and Granddad
would grumble back and forth about nothing, snippets of
conversation as necessary for flavor as the coffee and grease.

"Aunt Rosy and I played Rook the other night with
yer Granddad and it tickled us to beat him. He could hardly
stand it," Granny said to me, looking at Granddad. He kept
eating, ignoring what she'd said.

"Remember Odis? Aunt Ella's son?" Granny asked
me. "Got a letter from her, and she said he died. Had cancer,
but was converted before he died. Said he was ready to go; he
died singing a sacred song. He was a real good singer."

Granddad sipped his coffee. Nothing he had heard so
far seemed to require a comment from him. Then: "I'll tell ya
right now, war in fer some bad snow this year," he said, not

so much changing the subject as just deciding to talk. He judged the weather by the corns on his toes, the stiffness in his joints, and the fogs in August. He leaned over slowly to reach for his spit can, which sat conveniently behind the pot-belly stove. From his overalls pocket he pulled his tobacco twist and pinched off a wad. He liked to chew after supper and would carefully spit his juice with a "pffitt" into the can. His chair squeaked and the can "ting-ed" every time he spat.

Walter Napoleon Crain was seldom wrong about the weather, or anything else for that matter. The only thing he ever admitted to being wrong about was buying a 1920 Model-T truck. He had been more accustomed to driving wagons and mules than trucks, but he hadn't been able to resist the urge to own a real gas-powered vehicle. He had been hauling hogs in the back of his new truck and it was full of hog manure, so he took it to the river to wash out the bed. He backed the truck into a gravel pit that was near the river bank. Before he could do much washing, the gravel gave way and the truck started sinking into the river. The Current River was known for its swift water and undertow, and it quickly began to swallow the truck. Granddad jumped on top of the hood and grabbed a tree branch, clinging for his life because he had never learned to swim. The truck sank and was lost forever.

"Never did trust them dad-blame vehicles again ...Never owned another one in my life," he mumbled, sailing a stream of brown juice into his can.

I have been young, and now am old;
Yet I have not seen the righteous forsaken,
Nor his descendants begging bread.
He is ever merciful, and lends;
And his descendants are blessed.

Psalm 37:25

17

Seek, and Ye Shall Ride

W e entered Burley, Idaho, along with a freak, early
snow that didn't stick to the ground. This was only a
teaser of things to come. In mid-September winter was forc-
ing its way sooner than normal into this state of famous potatoes. And we had yet to cross the Cascade Mountains.

We walked within sight of the wide and beautiful
Snake River. Around us lay the most fertile fields of sugar
beets and potatoes in the world. Haystacks dotted the open
pastures, and we watched the flight of honking geese headed
south to warmer places. The temperature warmed to just
sixty degrees as we entered Twin Falls late one cloudy afternoon, just in time to eat a good meal. We would stay in a motel tonight because we did not have our winter sleeping bags.
They were being mailed to us here in Twin Falls, and we
needed them to sleep comfortably in the suddenly cooler
temperatures. The bags would keep us warm in weather as
cold as ten below zero.

"I want to spend some time with a real homesteader,"

Peter told me the next day. Idaho was a young state. Surely we could find some original or second generation folks who had made this land their own.

"How will we do that?" I asked.

"Don't know. Maybe somebody at the Chamber of Commerce can help."

After a few phone calls, Peter got the name of the bank vice president in Twin Falls, Jack Ramsey.

"Hello, Mr. Ramsey? My name is Peter Jenkins, and my wife and I are walking across America and..." Peter began to tell the whole story and what he wanted from Mr. Ramsey. He hoped the banker would introduce us to a family who had settled in the area from its earliest days. The man on the other end of the line seemed receptive, and the two talked for almost an hour.

"God's on the move!" Peter said when he hung up, his eyes sparkling with excitement.

"What did Mr. Ramsey say?" I was anxious.

"Let's get packed and ready to go. Mr. Ramsey has invited us to go with him and his wife to their cabin in the Sawtooth Mountains for the weekend."

"Peter, we don't know these people. How can we just take off with strangers?"

"Because this is from God."

Lucy Adele Dillingham Ramsey sat in the front seat of the big comfortable car as we headed north toward the mountains and their cabin. She was around sixty years old with curly white hair, pale milk skin, and a wry sense of humor. She had a continuous chuckle under her breath. She worked on a needlepoint project while her husband, Jack, drove, and her fingers were as quick and nimble as her wit. The work looked tedious to me, but Lucy loved it. She was working on a beautiful pillow cover for one of her friends.

Jack was easygoing, slow to say what he thought, and a perfect match for his witty, outspoken wife. He was close to retirement from the bank and was looking forward to traveling more if his heart condition would allow it. He kept a pipe in the corner of his mouth and made occasional puffs. The car smelled spicy, full of aroma.

Jack and Lucy were from a long line of Methodists and lived outside Twin Falls in a little town called Filer. All five of their children were grown. Jake, the oldest, was a banker like his dad, Camille was a teacher, Tom a policeman, Guy a carpenter, and Kirk, the youngest, was a clothes designer in San Francisco. Kirk had inherited his mother's artistic flair. There was something very special about Jack and Lucy. We were liking them more with each passing mile, beginning to feel like family in just one afternoon. They loved to be with younger people and sorely missed all their grown children. We gladly filled the vacancy.

This seemed like a dream. Just a few hours earlier we had been wondering what would happen to us here in Idaho, and with the blink of an eye, we were off on another adventure with people we had just met. Jack and Lucy told us they were apprehensive about inviting us to join them for the weekend.

"I did some checking... Found out you're who you said you were... Looked up the April '77 issue of *National Geographic* and sure enough, there was Peter Jenkins." Jack talked slowly. His voice was deep and soothing. He took a long draw on his pipe and grinned at us over his shoulder. "This is pretty nifty. And, I've found just the family of homesteaders you're looking for. Fine people. Hard working. And real cowboys. We'll drive by their ranch on the way back. Bill Williams is the name, he homesteaded his place with his wife, Viola, back at the turn of the century. Their two sons, Billy and Tommy, and their grandsons still run the place. That Williams outfit is a genuine operation and a good group of folks."

For the next month we would become a part of the Ramsey family and the Williams outfit. I would learn some things that would change my life forever.

"Yaw! Gitty-up!" "Yaw, Yaw!" "Git along there!" Shouting came from every direction. Cowboys were whistling, some were twirling lassos, and others were rounding up strays. I'd never seen so many cattle. And I'd never helped round them up either. But here we were, pushing two hundred cows, out on eighty-seven thousand acres with the Williamses and several other ranchers.

Peter and I were riding two of the more gentle horses, the kind that could stop short, cut quick, and knew how to work cattle. Peter's horse was called "Cougar" and mine was "Little Mister."

"Horses have got to have 'cow sense,' " Billy Williams said.

A dozen cowboys were on horseback with their lunches, canteens and chewing tobacco. I felt privileged to be a part of the group driving the herd down from the open range that bordered the south end of the Williams' ranch. There were thousands of acres of range for grazing cattle during the summer, and now the cows had to be rounded up and driven back to the ranch before winter. Although this was government land, a group of ranchers was permitted to graze it. They were called Western Stock Growers and some of the members were the Butlers, Williams, Crocketts, Kinseys, Browns, Morgans, and the Brockmans. Each member had a special date to take his cows out, and most of these folks were here today helping drive the Williams' cows home.

Dogs barked and nipped at the heels of stubborn calves. Cows bawled, horses snorted, men hollered. Dust filled the dry autumn air. Clouds and clouds of brown. Most of the cowboys wore handkerchiefs tied around their weathered faces, covering their noses and mouths. Unprepared, I squinted a lot and kept my mouth shut, until I borrowed a handkerchief from Charlotte Crockett.

This attractive rancher was around fifty years old

with short gray hair that peeked out from under her cowboy hat. She was strong and stocky. As a member of the association she had some of her cattle on this range. She'd been a rancher most of her life and had raised cattle alone since her husband's death fifteen years earlier. She showed me how to turn my horse, how to hold my body in the saddle so I wouldn't get so sore, and how to "yip" just right. At this point I didn't know I'd be in the saddle for twelve hours the first day.

Carol Ann Brockman Hopwood, a young cowgirl in her early twenties, rode up from behind on her horse, Toby. Carol was a newlywed, only married a little over a year, and she and her cowboy husband were the official caretakers of all these cattle while they grazed the open range. They lived in a secluded cow camp, nestled in rolling hills that separated Idaho from Nevada, from June to October every year, watching thousands of head of cattle.

"I like a clean house, cooking and stuff, but I still like to be out. I love to ride my horse and to work. Can't stand to sit around," Carol told me. She wore glasses, a long-brimmed baseball cap, and jeans. She seemed quiet, almost shy, but had a fast smile and ready laugh. She told me she was the assistant leader of the 4-H Club and taught young kids how to raise prize-winning cattle.

"Don't think I could live in town. I think townspeople are afraid of animals. Besides, I can't drive very well in all that traffic," she said. I laughed. To her, Twin Falls with one main street was like a metropolis.

Charlotte and Carol showed me how to keep my big mare under control. I was glad to hear we would be stopping at noon to eat our sack lunch, build a campfire, and wash down with coffee the dust we'd eaten all morning.

"Ever had cowboy coffee?" Charlotte asked.

"Can't say as I have. How's it different from ordinary coffee?" I asked.

"No different. Just put some grounds in a can of water, let it boil over a campfire, and ya got yourself some good coffee."

Carol and I were the only ones out here who didn't have on cowboy hats. I wore a floppy cotton hat, and Carol wore her baseball cap. I was going to make a comment about the cowboy hats when Carol's husband rode up next to us.

Rodney was the most genuine cowboy I'd ever seen, with his black hair, square jaw, unshaven face, and lanky body. He sat like an elegant statue on his horse, hands crossed on top of his saddle, his weathered boots anchored in the stirrups. He had just a pinch of Copenhagen snuff under his lip. There was nothing disturbed about this young cowboy. He belonged out here with the sagebrush, blue skies, and endless range. Rodney had started "cowboyin' " in Nevada at the Salmon River Cattlemen's Association, herding cows on 450,000 acres. This Idaho range was small in comparison. Carol had met Rodney when he started working here, for this association, where her father was a member.

"Rodney, maybe you can answer my question," I said. "Why are cowboy hats curved upward on the sides?"

Rodney never hurried about anything, especially talking. He thought a bit, straightened his lean back, then lifted his stirrups, ready to ride off. "So three cowboys can fit into a pickup truck."

Ask, and it will be given to you; seek, and you will find.
                                                    Matthew 7:7

18

Viola and Her Cowboys

The Williams' ranch was different from most others. The cowboys only had to open gates to let their herd out onto the range. And when they drove the cattle home in the fall, all they had to do was mount their horses and push the cows and calves down from the gulches and hills through the gates of the corrals. These cows did not have to be loaded into a semitruck to get them off the range and back home. They never saw a truck unless they were on their way to be sold.

The Williams owned at least ten thousand acres of deeded land that bordered the SawTooth Hills, where the cattle grazed during the summer. Besides cows they raised beans, wheat, corn, hay, and horses. Among the hundreds and hundreds of cows, there were many calves left without mothers to feed them. The mothers sometimes died while birthing a calf, were struck by lightning, or fell to some disease. This was when Viola stepped in. She took care of all orphaned newborn calves, as many as four at a time, and would bottle-feed them until they were old enough to graze.

171

Agnes Viola Green Williams was a powerhouse of a woman, yet she weighed only 110 pounds and stood not five feet tall. No one would have guessed she was seventy-two years old or that she had been married fifty years. Viola looked so much younger. She wore her long hair in a bun on top of her head and had it colored regularly.

She and her husband Bill had started out as sheepherders living in a log cabin with newspapers for wallpaper and cow patties for fuel. Sometimes sagebrush was needed for burning, but she preferred using it in the early years of marriage for Christmas trees.

"I'm a hillbilly, raised up in Soldier Creek. I married Bill when I was twenty-two," she said. She had a high-pitched voice. It quivered when she talked.

She had ridden a horse to school and attended through the eighth grade. She was the oldest child of eight and had helped with the younger children, picking potatoes, driving herds of horses, and rounding up cattle. She had worked hard all her life.

"I've always liked to live in the country, don't know what I'd do if I lived in town," Viola said.

"Seems pretty active around here on the ranch. Guess you really don't need to live in town for excitement," I said. Their white frame house sat on the edge of their land. From the back porch I could see the mountains dotting the horizon, seventeen miles away. The Williams owned all the land in between. Since we had come, there had been a constant flow of people in and out of their modest home. Grown sons, Billy and Tommy, ran most of the operation. Now, Bill and Viola's grandsons worked here, too. And there were between two and six hired men at all times. Whenever there was a lull in the back door's slamming, in came the milkman or neighbors. And Viola's cousin Alvin also lived with them.

"Bill and I have been married fifty years, and we've never been alone in our lives. We've always had someone living with us." That was hard for me to understand.

"We had an old mountain man who lived with us, Bill Sutton, for eight years. Then a little Italian man, Joe Lanzo, lived here three years. He visited us one time, then just stayed. And Alvin's here now," she said, looking over at the sad man who sat with slumped shoulders. He was an older fellow, never married, a mysterious person no one knew how to explain. He sat in the same chair, day after day, never talking. The only movements he made were to wipe the tears from his eyes.

"Sand, dust from ranchin' as a kid, ruined his eyes," Viola told me. "He's smart as a whip, just backward. Never was let off the ranch, grew up eating cereal for breakfast with water instead of milk, must have affected him." I forced myself not to look at Alvin, who heard every word she said. Although he would not respond to her most of the time, Viola directed many of her questions and comments toward him to include him. She treated him the same as the tough cowboys who stomped the manure off their boots before coming in her house to sit at her giant table of food.

Most of the time I was with Viola, I only wanted to ask her questions and listen. She had lived an extraordinary life, yet seemed not to know it. At her age she could still move circles around me.

"Two things I like to do. Fish and cook," Viola told me.

"I guess you like to see these working men eat a lot," I said.

"Oh, you bet. I've cooked for as many as sixteen men a day. Feel like I been cookin' all my life. I never like to go anywhere cause I don't like to leave my guys to care for themselves. I've always waited on my men. It's my duty."

Viola had no idea what I was thinking. She would never understand today's society of career-minded women who often think that cooking and "waiting on men" is common work, below one's potential, demeaning, and not professional. What bright college-educated young woman, even a Christian, would accept such a servant's role?

"Life's what you make it," Viola went on. "I remember washing clothes on a washboard, standing on a box cause I wasn't big enough. These younger people have too easy a life. Lord, if they'd had to live in times like me, they'd never a made it. We had to work like dogs and I never was lazy. I used to go like a whirlwind but the last couple of years, I can feel myself a laggin'."

She still seemed like a whirlwind to me, and I hoped I would have half her energy and spunk when I was seventy-two years old. After watching Viola busy at her endless common chores, and never complaining, I felt ashamed for whining about the inconveniences on our walk across America and especially about not having a servant's heart. She was teaching me so much about God without quoting one Scripture verse.

Viola's laminated round table was piled full of beef steaks, rolls, gravy, potato salad, Jell-O, deviled eggs, and jugs of iced tea. I helped set the plates and silverware. The radio phone sat on the countertop, near where she cooked. Over the noise of her rattling steaming pots, she could call the cowboys home from the range and the field hands in from the combines and get all her men fed properly.

But as for you, speak the things which are proper for sound doctrine: the older women likewise, that they be reverent in behavior, . . . teachers of good things.

Titus 2:1–3

19

A Wise Man Named Milo

Peter

J ohn Day, Oregon, isn't big, but it's big enough to be a city in the wild west. Every fall cowboys still drive herds of cattle fattened on mountain meadows right down Main Street. I'm talking about the wild west of the eighties, the 1980s.

Just about everyone in John Day knows a man named Milo Franke, who rides around on a Honda motorcycle. Milo thinks of himself as partially retired, now that he's only riding a "sedate" cycle. He used to ride one of the original "hawgs," an old Harley Davidson 74. "Seventy-four" definitely does not stand for the year it was made, since Milo rode it decades ago.

"Compared to a wild horse my motorcycle has a smooth ride," Milo says. Milo used to break wild horses, the harder-headed they were, the more Milo enjoyed it. "Being a rancher I got used to living outside, and I just love to feel that cool air rush by me as I'm going to visit one of my church members in the hospital or headed to jail to pray with someone."

This wise man named Milo has been a preacher of the gospel, pastoring churches throughout this sparsely populated section of central Oregon, for more than forty years. He's taller than six feet and has long white, lamb-chop sideburns and a handshake that you'd better be ready for if you want your hand back uncrushed. When Milo looks at you with his steady, blue eyes that are as clear and deep as a glacier lake, you get the feeling that Milo sees all that's inside of you.

Milo was different from any pastor or minister I'd ever met. Pastoring his flock was just one of his jobs. He and Evelyn, the love of his life, had also raised a bunch of children and tended cows, sheep, and horses on a ranch of ten thousand acres, which included a couple of canyons, forests, and high mountain pastures. Not only was Milo a preacher, a cowboy, a rancher, and an evangelist, but most of his life he had worked "full-time" in the logging woods cutting huge timber, easily one of the toughest jobs anywhere. Milo was also one of the world's great storytellers, and his were all true. He'd seen God do so much and had done so much himself there was no need to add anything to his memory.

Milo told me that when he was a young and energetic man, although he still had more energy than most thirty year olds, he would go to work before sunrise as a logger. He'd be through at about 3:30 P.M. in the summer. Then, before coming home to the ranch, he'd go to a site where he was building a new church. Sometimes Milo would work until 10 P.M. on that little country church, under lights strung over two-by-fours. Milo would tell his fellow loggers, many of whom were a hard-drinking bunch, that they needed to put some of their time into helping him build whatever church he was building at the time. Sure enough, before those tough men could make it to the Past-time Bar, they would be pounding nails and putting up the walls of the church.

Often Milo was so tired from working in the logging

woods and then on the church that he wouldn't even make it inside the house when he finally got back to the ranch. Milo would just step inside the gate and fall down in the yard. There he'd wake up the next morning, covered with an Oregon dew but rested just the same.

Other nights Milo would find himself riding one of his favorite horses home from a day in the mountains. He might be returning from bringing supplies to a sheep camp, high above. Soon he would spot the yellow-orange glow of lights in his family's small homeplace, cuddled far below in a narrow canyon. The only thing that Milo would rather have been doing was having an eternal effect on someone by leading him to Christ or baptizing him in water and the Holy Spirit.

This wise man pastored an Assembly of God church, and I'll never forget the Sunday morning in 1978 when he pointed at Barbara and me and said that God was speaking to him, telling him he should help us. As usual, Milo had on his black suit and looked like an old-time, wild-west, circuit-riding preacher. How did we need help, he wanted to know. I told him we were walking across America and that in the next month we would have to walk over the wilderness-covered Cascade mountains, in the middle of a deadly winter. He responded that he now knew why we needed him, and that without his help we would not make it across the mountains. In fact, we'd probably end up dead, frozen stiff as a fish, if we didn't have his help.

I've often wondered what would have happened to Barbara and me on our walk if we had been really stuck on one particular denomination instead of stuck on God. We might have told Milo, "Thanks, but you're not Baptist" or, "Thanks, but you're not Catholic or Church of Christ."

Milo was as close to God as anyone I'd ever met. And yet he was as realistic a person as I'd ever met. Unfortunately, at that point in my Christian life, I'd not met many who were a lot of both. Milo was unique. He would go for walks in the wild parts of the canyons and rim rock and see a weed, and God would bring a Scripture to him for next Sunday's sermon. One thing Milo used to say to me a lot was, "I love the sinner just as much as I love the church people. The thing I don't like is sin." Anyone who ever met this wise man sensed that. He'd give you the shirt off his back if you really needed it or be at your side, no matter who you were, if you needed prayer or comforting. He'd go to the local jail and reach out to a drunk as caringly as he would to the richest rancher in the valley laid up in a hospital bed. Both might have cursed Milo and God when they were healthy, and they might not have gone to his church, but when they really needed God, they knew to call for Milo. I wanted to be as much like him as I could.

Milo did escort us across those mountains. The weather was so frigidly brutal that the elk came down from higher elevations to the valleys of the humans. Barbara was pregnant and sick and didn't want to talk much, but as we trudged along, Milo creeping beside us in his Chevrolet pickup, I couldn't ask him enough questions. Plus, being with Milo, no matter where we were, was like being at a perpetual party, except that Milo wasn't high on drugs or booze but on the Holy Spirit. I marveled at all he'd been through and seen. I prayed that I would be as vital and pumped up as he was after being a Christian for so many decades.

As the temperature dropped way below zero and the snowflakes got as big as pine cones, Milo told us stories, hoping to keep us inspired. As usual he had on his black cowboy hat and black western jacket. I'd ask him a question, he'd answer, and I would ask another. He always cut through the "jive of life" with his parable-like answers.

One thing I wanted to know more about was TV preachers. I had a great curiosity about these personalities on TV who had big ministries, who took in all that money. Were they all doing pure good, as some folks thought? Or were they all bad, as others said? I was confused, and I wondered if Milo could clear this up for me. Many times I found myself feeling something other than purity and light coming from the big-time preachers, but I felt guilty for thinking anything but the best about their million-dollar ministries. I was bothered by people who said, "I love the Lord," and who presented an image of perfection but still didn't ring true in what they said and did.

Milo responded to my questions with another of his Scripture-inspired stories. "Peter," he said, "I'm nothing but a fruit inspector."

"A fruit inspector! Come on, Milo," I said, my breath puffing small clouds as I laughed. Milo was known for his joking. "What do you mean?"

"Peter, seriously, you must learn to be a fruit inspector, as I've had to. Don't just listen to what they say or notice how good they look. Never put too much stock in how much education they've got. Don't rely solely on who's got the biggest church, shiniest car, or fastest computer." Milo glanced up into a snow-covered ponderosa pine. "I've been with some of the most 'famous' preachers and evangelists in America, and I've been with some of the least known people, too. Some people can say all the right things, quote all the right Scriptures, and appear just 'perfect.' But they may be bearing the most rotten fruit. Or they may be bearing abundant fruit, their tree hanging heavy."

Barbara came alive when she overheard this story. "Peter, honey," she said, "this whole thing is inspired by the Book of Matthew. I love those particular Scriptures so much." Her steps through the deep snow quickened. "I'm not sure we've ever read them together."

Milo jumped out of his truck, stood in the foot-deep snow with us, and quoted from memory from the Book of Matthew.

" 'Beware of false prophets, which come to you in sheep's clothing, but inwardly they are ravening wolves. You will know them by their fruits. Do men gather grapes from thornbushes or figs from thistles?' " Snowflakes caught on Milo's long gray sideburns. Holy fire flashed in his light blue eyes.

" 'Even so, every good tree bears good fruit, but a bad tree bears bad fruit. A good tree cannot bear bad fruit, nor can a bad tree bear good fruit. Every tree that does not bear good fruit is cut down and thrown into the fire.' I've seen some of the holiest looking trees cast into the fires!" Milo shouted.

"Therefore by their fruits you will know them!" Milo could take no more. He was preaching in our church of ponderosa pines, carpeted wall-to-wall with fresh snow.

Milo took my face in his preacher's hands. "Peter, you must never forget this; you must learn to be a fruit inspector! Always walk through the orchard and inspect the fruit."

by their fruits you will know them!

20

The Great Waters

The temperature had plunged to just two degrees. I had never slept outside in such cold weather, but our down sleeping bags and glacier tent kept us snug and warm. Crawling out of the bags at sunrise, our breath white like steam, was hard, but up the road was a town where we could get hot coffee and breakfast.

Oregon was cold but clean. The roadsides were immaculate, no beer cans or empty soda bottles. The ditches held icy water but no trash or leftovers from fast-food restaurants. We were moving slowly across a high plateau in central Oregon when it began to snow. Flakes as big as feathers from thick, gray clouds. There was nothing to do but take one step at a time, plugging forward with our heads down to keep snow out of our faces. A quietness blanketed us like the snow. This was a perfect time to savor memories and think about the end of our walk. It wouldn't be long now. Only weeks.

Peter and I had come so far together. We had lived through more unusual experiences in two years together than

181

many couples do in a lifetime. The thoughts popped in and out of my head as I fought back a sick feeling in my stomach. I couldn't understand why I had been feeling so poorly lately. Phrases from Scriptures came to mind—"And let us not grow weary while doing good...But those who wait on the LORD shall renew their strength...All things work together for good...To everything there is a season"—*Even ending our walk*, I thought. I hoped the mental cheerleading would make me feel better and help me keep plodding through the wet snow.

We were walking on a high ridge, flat and open to the snowy winds, when a pickup stopped. There was little traffic out here other than the rural-route mail carrier. He introduced himself as Lawrence McCracken.

"I cover more than a hundred miles a day on this route," he told us. He was a middle-aged man, tall, husky, but not threatening. He talked gently and had tender eyes. Reaching for a thermos he asked if we wanted something to warm us up. We climbed into the cab and warmed our faces in the steam of the hot coffee. This was a welcome surprise. Mr. McCracken had passed us on the road for several days and had been keeping an eye on us.

"Want a Fig Newton?" he asked. We tried not to grab the chewy cookies out of his hand.

We learned that he and his wife, Trudy, had children our age and that she often rode with him on his mail route. Mr. McCracken was concerned about our being out on the road in this bad weather. We assured him we would be all right. We told him one story after another of how God had cared for us while crossing America, stories about receiving money, food, water in Utah, a cabin to live in for the winter in Colorado, and protection from outlaws and snakes. We became thankful all over again just remembering all the ways God had intervened on our behalf.

"Bless the LORD, O my soul, and forget not all His benefits," I said, quoting the Scripture verse from Psalms as a reminder to Peter and myself. We both had been guilty of forgetting how much God had done for us.

Just as we finished the last cookie, the heavy gray clouds parted and a stream of white rays shone down, a funnel of light illuminating the road. The three of us sat there without saying a word, awestruck by the quiet beauty coming out of the heavens.

Mr. McCracken took off his glasses and pulled out his handkerchief. I had supposed the steam from the coffee had covered his lenses, but I saw tears brimming in his eyes.

"I made a mistake when I told you about my children," Mr. McCracken said, his voice breaking.

"What do you mean?" Peter said.

"I really have two more, named Peter and Barbara." Tears started to roll down his kind face. "I may not have as much faith as I should, but it's always good to hear how God takes care of others."

We climbed out of his truck and strapped on our gear. This moment would always stand out in my memory.

"God bless you, Mr. McCracken," Peter said as they shook hands.

"He already has," he said.

John Day, Oregon, became an eventful town for us. On December 2, at 11:09 A.M., we received the following telegram:

I am enthusiastic and honored to join you for the successful conclusion of your great journey. Your accomplishment ranks with the best in the *Geographic's* long tradition of encouraging and supporting explorers and adventurers. Admittedly, your adventure was a long shot at the beginning, but I had every confidence that you would follow through until you reached your goal. From the very offset, we at *Geographic* expected much more from you than just a walk across America, and

you have not disappointed us. Best Regards, Gilbert M.
Grosvenor, *National Geographic*

Peter and I jumped up and down with happiness.
They were coming! The editor and other staff members from
the *National Geographic* headquarters in Washington were
coming to join us for the end of the walk. We had written old
friends, family, and many we had met on the walk—practically everyone we knew—and invited them to join us to walk
the last mile.

We had mapped out our course and how long it
would take us to go from John Day to the coast. After some
soul-searching Peter and I had agreed it would be selfish for
us to end our walk alone. The people we had met along the
way throughout the past five years were what had made the
walk special. They were the life and breath of this land; they
were who God had chosen to guide us, to help us, to reveal
Himself to us. They deserved to share in the conclusion of
our adventure.

We thought at least two hundred people would come
from all over America. Our newest friends, Jack and Lucy
Ramsey, were coming. Even Bill, Viola, and the Williams
boys were taking a day off from the ranch. From as far east
as North Carolina and Alabama friends would be arriving.
Friends Peter had made on the first half of his walk, before
we met, were coming: M.C. and Margaret Jenkins, Mary
Elizabeth and Eric, and Carl and Clarice Henderson. Rita
Hauptman and Teddy were coming from New Orleans; Rev-
erend Green, his wife, Barbara, and their son, Michael. Gary
and Jean Wysocki from Colorado. Perk and Emma Jean.
Welch Hill. All the Jenkins clan, my parents and only sister,
Vicky. Don and Sarah Stevens and their children, Douglas
Glen and Sara Lee, from Dallas, Milo and Evelyn Franke,
Mike and Mary Lou Koto.

The list went on and on. Peter and I couldn't believe
so many people cared enough to drive or fly out to Oregon

just to walk one short mile with us. We guessed everyone knew what that mile meant to us, the last of more than 4,750 miles.

Even my one living grandma, Viola Louise Pennell, was coming. Grandma was eighty-three, had a heart condition, and lived in Phoenix, Arizona, but she asked her doctor for special permission to fly to Oregon. She would walk between Peter and me to set the pace for everyone else.

January 18, 1979, the day of our final mile. The weatherman predicted rain but the clouds pulled back and let the sun shine. The air was crisp, but not bitterly cold—more like a chilly fall day than mid-January. Everything was perfect. People laughed. There was a thrill in the air, and a sense of anticipation as the crowd walked behind Grandma, Peter, and me. The great waters of the Pacific were just ahead. We crossed the last sand dune and unlocked our hands from Grandma's. She had been singing the old church hymn, "The Last Mile of the Way," and faith and courage seemed to pass from her hands to ours, giving us one last boost as we approached the ocean's white, foamy surf.

Peter and I moved away from the crowd and walked, almost ran, to the edge of the water. We'd done what we'd set out to do, and much more. We'd finished what God had called us to do back in November, 1975, and in a very important way all of the people standing behind us were a part of that call.

The group began to clap and cheer, rejoicing with us, as we stepped into the icy water. We kept on walking right up to our waists. Feelings as powerful as the waves surging against us rolled through me. I wanted to yell, shout, and holler as loud as I could, "Praise the Lord! Praise the Lord! Praise the Lord!" But instead of whooping, I raised my arms in victory, embracing the whole sky and ocean until Peter grabbed me and gave me the last hug and kiss of the walk. Our tears and laughter blended together. We'd made it.

Now, we were to be blessed with a child, conceived on the walk. And we would have other adventures, sharing our lives and the America we'd found. Sharing the God we loved.

He has shown you, O man, what is good; and what does the LORD require of you but to do justly, to love mercy, and to walk humbly with your God?

Micah 6:8

21

Wildly Evil

Peter

S pring in New Orleans is a pleasant time of the year. A calm, cool time. Barbara and I were settled down for the first time, with one child, Rebekah, not yet two, a house with redwood siding, and a '72 VW that was a dull red, faded by the southern sun. I'd been cutting the grass all afternoon with the new push mower I'd bought a few weeks ago at Sears. Even though there was an acre to mow, I'd decided that I'd feel too lazy if I got a riding lawn mower. Besides, we couldn't afford a riding lawn mower. Barbara came out and gave me a quart jar filled with unsweetened iced tea and said that it was time to get ready for church.

We pulled into the parking lot of the Word of Faith, our church. The building was built out of cinderblocks painted white and the sanctuary was eight-sided. We'd heard our pastor, Reverend Charles Green, say many times that God had told him to buy the five acres the church was on when it was nothing but a dirt road and swamp. Now it was some of the most valuable real estate in the entire city.

Word of Faith was located about a half mile off the interstate right next to a sprawling shopping center called Lake Forest Mall and the Methodist Hospital. The Sunday night crowd was always smaller than Sunday morning's but usually there were at least six hundred folks at this service. Although it was a thirty-five mile drive one way, we felt it was more than worth it. We never left a service in which we hadn't been inspired by God and His Word.

I had noticed since we'd been going to church at Word of Faith that we often pulled into the parking lot at about the same time as certain other families. I'd usually see George and Jackie Dantin's partially rusted-out, dull-green station wagon, which they called "Lurch," looking for a roomy space. Bud and Sandy always seemed to park by the side door, maybe because Sandy didn't want her hairdo to blow away. The Bakers didn't care where they parked but were always unloading their river of children.

Most of the people who were heading into church had Bibles and babies in their arms. This was a congregation with a lot of young families. Somebody once told me that you can always tell a really "growing and going" church, no matter which denomination, by how many young people and men it has in it.

I opened the door for Barbara and Rebekah and also held it for Garlon Pemberton. Garlon, an associate pastor, had grown up tough in Texas. The man had a square build, and his muscles and voice were filled with power. Before becoming a preacher he'd been a boxer, and he was so full of energy he could have sold the excess to the power company. Garlon was loved by everyone and must have been in his early sixties—although no one ever thought about how old he was.

We usually sat on the left side of the sanctuary, about halfway to the front. Comfortable blue theater seats were our pews. People dressed casually on Sunday nights, some of the men in nice shirts and slacks and some of the women in pants. It was the kind of service in which the preachers and the people often found themselves laughing at something funny.

Sometimes the pastor's son, Michael Green, would make some contorted face while leading the choir. Michael, I'm sure, had spent most of his twenty-five-odd years in church. He was blond, an excellent singer, and had a semi-irreverent sense of humor. It was more or less irreverent depending on how well Michael thought you could take a joke, and he always seemed to know the latest jokes going around the country. Michael was single, drove a beautiful Buick Riviera, and wore foreign-made sunglasses. At one time or another all the young girls at church had a crush on him.

Garlon usually preached on Sunday nights, and after a special song by Michael called "Rise Again" by Dallas Holm, Brother Garlon casually walked to the podium and announced there would be a baptism tonight. This church believed in total immersion, not sprinkling as did the First Presbyterian Church of Greenwich, Connecticut, where I got my first exposure to Christianity.

Walking down the stairs from both sides of the baptismal waters were Garlon and David Newwell, another associate pastor. David was a small, scholarly young man and a graduate of Princeton Theological Seminary. The pastors always seemed to walk so slowly as they headed into the waters of baptism, which heightened the drama of the moment. Garlon said that tonight a woman wanted to be baptized; her name was such and such. I'd never seen her before, but she appeared to be in her midfifties, had brown hair, was dressed quite well, and looked like someone who'd put in thirty years at a government office. She walked down into the water with them.

Being baptized by being fully "immersed," means standing in a large tank filled with water, or if your church can't afford a heated tank, being taken under in a creek or pond. I'd heard that out in California some of the churches had mass baptisms in someone's swimming pool. Anyway, the idea is that every bit of your body has to be covered with water. When the preacher lowers you into the water it means that your old self, the you before you made the decision to believe in Jesus, is dying and being buried and when you rise out of the water you're being raised from the dead. I'd been baptized in this church right before we'd left on our walk back in 1976.

Rebekah was fidgety tonight, tearing up the program into tiny pieces. I found myself thinking about the alligator we'd seen while driving to church that morning. The huge thing had crossed the interstate and three trucks had almost hit it.

Garlon, David, and the woman were now waist deep in the heated water. Garlon was standing behind her and David was standing in front. Garlon put his hand on her forehead and whispered, "Now hold your breath, this won't take long." His voice got louder. "Upon the profession of your faith in the Lord Jesus Christ and in obedience to His command, I now baptize you in the name of the Father, the Son, and the Holy Ghost."

At this point I reached down to pick up Barbara's purse, which Rebekah had just upended. Our checkbook fell under the row in front, and I had to strain to get it. Now the woman was baptized, but instead of walking out, dripping wet, she began talking to Garlon. Her voice sounded strange. "I know God as well as you do!" she said. This was very unusual. Everyone who had not been quiet, now was.

Garlon paused, slightly surprised. He told her to say, "Jesus is my Lord." She wouldn't say anything. "I command you to identify yourself!" shouted Garlon. He seemed to be speaking to something or someone other than the woman. Nothing was said. I could hear the sounds of prayer in the congregation. Rebekah scrambled into my lap.

Then this woman, who'd looked so normal and proper, lunged through the water and threw David up against

Very touching!
+ scary -

the walls of the baptistry. He hit with a thud. A loud sound came out of her, like the growl of a wolf. *This can't be happening*, I thought. Rebekah gripped my arm as hard as her little hands could. Foam was coming out of the woman's mouth. She whirled around and headed for Garlon. "Her eyes were wildly evil," he told me later.

"I know you," Garlon spoke to her or whatever was in her, "and I speak to you in the name of Jesus Christ your Master. I will not compromise, you must come out of her and go back to the pit." The sounds of praying voices were as loud as the ocean. The woman's voice took on a shrill, mocking tone, then she started screaming and jabbering. David had recovered his balance and held out his right hand toward her, praying, I guessed. Everyone's eyes were glued to the baptistry.

"This woman is like the slave girl Paul wrote about in the sixteenth chapter of Acts, the one who had the spirit of divination," Garlon said. "Everybody pray!"

The woman's "voice" then became very low, like a man's deep bass voice, and she said some foul words I never thought I'd hear in church. I hadn't cared to see any of the movies that dealt with demons and witchcraft, but now it seemed I was witnessing the real thing.

Garlon repeated, "Say Jesus is my Lord."

She said nothing. Garlon repeated it again, forcefully. "Say Jesus is my Lord!"

Finally, she whimpered, "Jesus is my Lord."

The moment she spoke her body went completely limp and she almost slumped down under the water before the two preachers could lift her up and out of the baptistry. Some women escorted her to a changing room and helped her get dressed. We found out later that week that the woman had been deeply involved in the practice of voodoo and other occult activities for many years.

Garlon and David took their wet clothes off, put their suits back on, and came out onto the platform. Garlon walked up to the microphone, paused a moment, and said, "I love a good fight."

————————————

Now John answered Him, saying, "Teacher, we saw someone who does not follow us casting out demons in Your name, and we forbade him because he does not follow us."

But Jesus said, "Do not forbid him, for no one who works a miracle in My name can soon afterward speak evil of Me. For he who is not against us is on our side."

Mark 9:38–40

22

Date Night

Peter

One of the most important things God has taught Barbara and me is something we call "date night." Every Tuesday night Barbara and I go out on a date. Sometimes we go to a movie. Recently we saw "Witness" and loved it. Or we go out to eat. Often we don't want to be around other people, so we climb in my pickup truck and just cruise down the beautiful country roads that go in every direction here in middle Tennessee.

We're strange because we especially like to ride around when a big blizzard's blowing in, or during torrential downpours, or when the winds are stiff and whipping. We'd rather watch the drama of the weather, with the Lord's winds and rain as the sound-track, than find some form of man-made entertainment.

The most important thing about our date night is being *together*. No kids, no friends, no family, no pets. We've both realized that as our responsibilities have increased—children, writing, running a farm, going to church and Sunday school, speaking all over the USA, changing the oil in

193

our cars, having people working for us, and more and more—that we have to *make* time to be alone.

Barbara and I learned that building a solid Christian marriage meant more than being in church every time the doors were open, more than enjoying the fellowship of others, more than reading the Bible and praying. It meant being together, and not just late at night when the house was quiet with the soft sounds of sleeping children and exhausted parents half-awake. We needed to give ourselves the best hours of at least one day.

So after being married for seven years we started dating again. This has kept us from being *just* married parents who have kids, who live on a farm, who write books, and who go on adventures. It's kept us friends.

"BJ, where do you want to go tonight?" Every other date night, BJ (I call Barbara that sometimes) decides where she wants to go, *even* if it means going shopping (Blah!).

"I thought it would be fun to hop into the pickup and go down to the Sonic," she said. The Sonic is a drive-in at Lewisburg, a neighboring town, where they make great chilidogs and onion rings.

"That sounds great. I'm not in the mood to be around a bunch of people," I said. I'd just come home from four days of speaking at some colleges in Michigan.

Usually Barbara won't get into the truck until I clean out the seat. On her side might be anything from hamburger wrappers to needles I've used giving a sick cow a shot. Sometimes I have to cover the seat with a sheet if Barbara's wearing some of her good clothes.

Oh, no, I thought, realizing the truck had never looked so grungy, dusty, and junked up. Her side of the floor was littered with string from hay bales, pieces of barbed wire from a fence repair job, and some stained coffee cups I hadn't brought back inside the house. I wondered if any penicillin mold could be growing on her side of the truck.

"What's wrong, Peter?" Barbara asked, wondering why I wasn't on my way to get the pickup. I was startled when a mockingbird flew out of the grapevine next to me.

"Are you sure you want to go in the truck? And if you are, you'd better wear your jeans 'cause I don't think I can get it clean enough before we have to leave." I didn't even want to think about what might be in the *back* of the truck.

My truck may be dirty but I love it. I enjoy the fact that I don't have to keep it clean. In fact, when I'm riding in it I feel like a ten-year-old boy again, and it seems only natural that there should be dust on the seats and hay in the back. Normally, my axe, shotgun and tree-pruners are behind the seat.

"I'm in a goin' to the drive-in, listenin' to country music, and wearin' blue jeans mood, anyway, cowboy," Barbara said flirtatiously. She was very proud of her "country-girl" roots and was thrilled that I was slowly becoming such a "country boy."

She might have wanted to look like a country girl, ready for a night of fun, but I knew her mood was far more serious when she said that she had something to talk about. Oftentimes, when BJ has something we need to talk about, like disciplining the children or my occasional insensitivity to her, she approaches the topic in the way a Sunday school teacher would teach a lesson. She gets all prepared for our "class." Sometimes to support her "lesson," she has a book or an article we need to read.

Other times she has in her orderly mind exactly *what* she wants us to talk about and *how* we need to progress. I'm more accustomed to flowing from one thing to another, so we usually end up drifting along in a semiorganized state. Of course, that's after almost ten years of marriage. In the beginning I'd wanted *only* to flow and Barbara had wanted *only* to stay within her organization—she'd wanted to be serious about everything and I'd wanted to joke about everything.

"Honey, let's flashback on the last ten years since

you've become a Christian and talk about what you think are some of the important things God's taught you, okay?" she asked, sounding excited.

Barbara was always enthusiastic when she wanted to talk about the things of God. I put the pickup into reverse, watching carefully that none of our puppies was around. The puppies were usually everywhere, and they especially liked to be where they weren't supposed to be, like under the truck or chasing our calves.

Before we had reached the end of our gravel driveway, I had pushed the rewind button on my memory. Depending on how I viewed it, sometimes the last ten years looked like a sprint, sometimes like sleepwalking, and occasionally like I had been trying to hide my head in the sand. Most of the time it played back as an orderly, step-by-step spiritual journey.

"I'd have to say that one of the most important things I've learned is that God wants to educate us in a step-by-step progression," I said. Strong March winds blew and bent the supple branches of the poplar trees that grew on the creek banks we were passing.

"You know," I went on, "I used to get so anxious about wanting to learn everything immediately. Then I realized that it took a lot of time and that I had to work out certain things before I could go on to the next thing."

"Do you think that you were so anxious because you were raised a Yankee?" Barbara joked. "The way you used to be you wanted everything to happen yesterday. Ya really have slowed down, darlin', do ya realize that?" she said in her most sugary southern accent.

"Whatever youse says, dear," I said, switching to my best New York City cab driver accent, trying to sound hyper. We often gave each other a hard time about my Northern roots and her Southern ones.

I kept talking. "I think our taking things step by step applies to everything in life—our relationship with God, our marriage, making friends, building a house."

I shifted the truck into overdrive as we passed Dot and Horace Murphy's house. They lived about four miles from us on a small farm at the edge of a cedar woods. The moon was almost full, and the light from it turned all the fields we passed a chilled blue. I talked on, my eyes peering straight ahead, wary of deer that often leapt across the road.

"During the walk I knew there was no other way to make it across America than to put one foot in front of the other and take the joys and the pains and the worries as they came. That way everything was much easier to handle," I remembered. I still lived my life that way.

"When we were crossing the mountain ranges of Colorado I learned that I couldn't worry about who or what we'd run into a week farther up the trail, because if I didn't concentrate on where we were at the time, there might not be that next week. If I'd looked only at getting—" I stopped in the middle of a sentence as I swerved to miss a doe in the road. "—to the top of the mountain, I might have been overwhelmed and given up, but instead I took that mountain one step at a time."

I never can get enough of the conversations Barbara and I have. We love to talk to each other, a strong point of our relationship. Sometimes we talk for hours about "significant" topics. Other times we ride along for an hour and say nothing. Now that we have three children younger than six, talking at home is usually to one of the children along the lines of "Jed, do *not* color the sofa with the black felt-tip pen" or "Beka, honey, you need to take four more bites of that chicken." Talking to Luke is pure baby talk, "OO-key, how my 'ittle boy do-in?"

Barbara pushed the lever on the heater to high. The spring night air was chilly. "I used to think that living the Christian life sounded boring and too predictable," I went on. "But when God's leading your steps and He asks you to step into a situation that challenges you beyond what you thought possible, then it's anything but boring."

Barbara moved closer to me. The moonlight illumi-
nated the rippling surface of a slow-moving creek. We drove
by a dairy cow that was standing in the middle of the road,
chewing her cud. Barbara was really being quiet tonight, letting me do most of the talking. I put my arm around her
shoulder.

It occured to me that I'd learned a lot about God in
the past decade because I'd known almost nothing when I
came to Him. If anyone had asked me questions about the
Bible, I probably would have said that Timothy was my
friend from junior high, that Ruth was the only Jewish girl in
my fifth grade class, and the Acts was some new government
program to help the disadvantaged. "Praying" was for little
kids and grandmothers, and "fellowship" was something fra-
ternities did in some secret rite.

"One thing I remember being surprised at and being
confused about at first was the fact that there were so many
different types of Christians," I said. Since then I had come to
believe that God allowed us to have so many different
denominations to provide all His people with the places
where they could worship.

"I was really surprised when I first heard that some
Christians believe God still heals people. Some think that
every once in a while God heals someone of cancer, and
some believe that God heals people all the time—all you have
to do is ask and believe it's going to happen. Then there are
lots of Christians who think the last time there was any di-
vine healing done was when Jesus did it two thousand years
ago.

"During our years walking across America and all the
years since, I guess we've experienced just about every type
of Christian imaginable," I said.

"You've really learned a lot, Peter Jenkins," she said,
sounding impressed. "Honey, it amazed me how little you
knew. I mean, I grew up with it. Maybe someday you'll begin
really studying the Bible."

Of all the areas of my Christian life, I knew that I was least "together" about studying the Bible regularly. Barbara used to harass me about this until she read in one of Dr. Dobson's books that this kind of strategy wouldn't work, especially on someone like me. Nowadays she just playfully harassed me every once in a while, like every hour on the hour. (No, not really. She was letting God work on that weakness of mine.)

I saw three falling stars in a row. I loved this stretch of road because there were very few farmhouses and everything was very dark. We passed a barn that was lit up, and I wondered if the farmer was delivering a calf or nursing a sick horse.

"I may not have known much about Christianity," I said, "but I sure knew a lot more about cars and rock and roll than you did." I remembered when we'd first met, asking Barbara if she'd ever heard Jimi Hendrix and she hadn't. Then later that same day a Rolls Royce drove by and I mentioned that I would love to go for a ride in one. Barbara wanted to know how we could get a ride in Roy's "Royce." Besides, she didn't know I knew someone named Roy... Barbara didn't pay attention to *things* like cars and houses and clothes and rock and roll.

Barbara wanted to know how much farther we had to go. It looked like we had about five miles.

"You know, B.J., I'll never forget first hearing about the Second Coming," I said. "Now that was something I'd never heard about before walking through the Bible Belt. It seemed most Christians believed He was coming back, but that no one knew the place and time. Many thought we were living in the "end times," and others didn't think there was any need to worry because if you lived "right," the way a Christian was supposed to, then you'd be ready when He returned."

We were headed down the hill now. "You know, sometimes I feel like I'm missing out on all the 'fun' the unbelievers have. But then I remember that I've already lived that lifestyle and that it's nothing but groping in the dark for love and acceptance. And it usually ends up in hurt, hangovers, and pain."

I was glad I was no longer involved in that lifestyle. Talking now about my past, I found it amazing that I was so happy just riding in a pickup truck, headed for a little country town to eat chilidogs and onion rings.

We drove along the silent, dark, back roads of Tennessee, toward our "romantic" dinner at the drive-in. There would be no candlelight, just the speaker box to place our order. Somehow I felt a great comfort knowing there was *no way* to remember everything God had taught me, whether on a short ride in our truck or in a very big eternity.

Before I ordered I said, "We could drive around the world and never talk about all God is and all He's done. I don't think anyone is capable of comprehending all of Him. But I'm sure excited about trying to. I plan on following Him and asking Him for directions as long as I live. For me there's no other way."

"Me, too," Barbara said.

I ordered a chilidog with cheese and onion and two orders of onion rings and Barbara ordered one with just chili. She didn't order any onion rings but I knew she'd be eating some of mine. She did!

On the way home we talked about the latest "incredible" things the kids had been doing. Jed was close to being potty trained but did not have it figured out yet, while Rebekah had just learned to feed some grass to Shocker without being afraid. And the major new excitement of our week was that Luke was now able to hold his bottle. Wow!

We were full, filled with good fast-food, filled with the comfort of our togetherness, and filled with a powerful awareness of our relationship with God. We rode home quietly. All we heard were the sounds of the soft night air blowing by the truck.

Jesus answered and said to him, "Are you the teacher of Israel, and do not know these things?

"Most assuredly, I say to you, We speak what We know and testify what We have seen, and you do not receive Our witness. If I have told you earthly things and you do not believe, how will you believe if I tell you heavenly things? No one has ascended to heaven but He who came down from heaven, that is, the Son of Man who is in heaven.

read it again

"And as Moses lifted up the serpent in the wilderness, even so must the Son of Man be lifted up, that whoever believes in Him should not perish but have eternal life. For God so loved the world that He gave His only begotten Son, that whoever believes in Him should not perish but have everlasting life. For God did not send His Son into the world to condemn the world, but that the world through Him might be saved.

"He who believes in Him is not condemned; but he who does not believe is condemned already, because he has not believed in the name of the only begotten Son of God. And this is the condemnation, that the light has come into the world, and men loved darkness rather than light, because their deeds were evil. For everyone practicing evil hates the light and does not come to the light, lest his deeds should be exposed. But he who does the truth comes to the light, that his deeds may be clearly seen, that they have been done in God."

John 3:10–21

23

My Son

Peter

At the beginning of every spring, summer, fall, and winter I always think about why I love living in a part of the country that has four distinct seasons. For me, living with four changing seasons is like having four different personalities; I get to trade one in for another every three months.

When winter passes I think of the times just spent that I appreciated being inside, warmed by the wood fires in our black, cast-iron stove. Reading books, thinking deeply, and feeling the chilled loneliness of the winter landscape are special parts of my winter. I also love the cold, clean sounds of my boots crunching snow as I head for our barn loft about fifty yards from our house. Every December, January, and February day I must climb up there and pitch hay bales down to feed our cattle and Shocker, our six-year-old stallion. The sound of the winds moaning through the nail holes of the barn's roof and the cold, sweet smells of the hay make every winter day begin so fresh and alive. I love what cold weather does to me and the earth and my family. But after three months I'm ready for something else, namely spring.

When spring eases closer, life inside our farmhouse naturally moves outside. We can't wait to see the earth's coming back to color—the green of clover and the yellow daffodils. The rounded buds of the poplar trees on the creek revive us, and spring's brand-new and colorful life inspires us to wear colorful clothes, too. During the birthing of this new season, we are like animals peeking out from inside our den where we'd been so secure. A few weeks earlier we had only wanted to be outside when we absolutely had to. But now we want to be inside only when we have to. Barbara opens every window wanting the freshness of spring to come in and chase away the stale air of winter.

The pickup truck bounced as we drove through the pastures. My left arm hung out the window, warmed by the late March sun. I felt so good. Without warning a hand touched, then rested on my shoulder. The hand was strong yet soft. It was Jed's hand, my two-year-old son's hand. I never thought that a hand, just resting on my shoulder, could have such a powerful and wonderful impact on me.

Jed and I were just riding around, supposedly to see if any of the cows had had a calf. But that was only an excuse to be together. Never had I felt so close to another male as I did to Jed. Everyone said that he was a "Daddy's boy." He had extra big hands like his Grandpa Ernie and extra wide feet. He reminded me of my dog Cooper in his puppy days, when "Coop's" paws looked like they were two times too big for his body.

When Barbara was pregnant for the second time, a lot of our friends asked me if I wanted a boy or a girl. I'd say that it didn't matter as long as the baby was healthy. But down deep, as deep as my toes, I wanted this child to be a boy. I had no idea what difference it would make to have a boy, as opposed to having another girl, but I felt the strongest prehistoric urges. In fact, I wanted to keep going till we had at least one boy, which made both of us nervous since Barbara had said she only wanted to have two children.

To Jed it didn't matter whether it was day or night. Whenever I was getting ready to go anywhere, Jed would run up to me and say, "GO TOO!" Sometimes he could go with me and sometimes he couldn't. When he couldn't go with me, it always broke his little heart, and he'd cry and grab hold of my legs with a grip of surprising strength. Sometimes we'd have to peel him off me. Jed probably didn't realize that it hurt me deeply, too, when we couldn't be together. I'd try not to show how much it cut my heart.

When Jed could come with me he wanted to do whatever Daddy did. If I went out to feed Shocker and didn't act the least bit afraid of the "huge," black stallion, then Jed would feel he should be fearless also. "Shocky," he called to the horse just like me. My little buddy was very brave as long as my big body was between him and feisty Shocker. Life was filled with big, frightening things that didn't seem so big and frightening when Jed was right next to his father.

One spring day I told Jed to wait for me by the gate to Shocker's pasture because the ground was very muddy. No sooner had I walked into the barn than I heard Jed screaming. I knew that he'd opened the gate and tried to follow. I looked out to see Shocker running full speed right at him, an avalanche of black.

Fortunately, Shocker skidded to a halt when he heard Jed crying and screaming. Knowing Shocker as well as I do, I'm sure he was just playfully teasing Jed and then realized that he couldn't play with him the way he plays with me! Shocker calmly turned and walked over to me. Shocker had a look on his face that said he would never try that again with such a small human being. Jed wouldn't move, so I picked him up and he petted Shocker's nose before we closed the gate to the pasture. Shocker acted as sweet as he could be.

Just about everything that has happened between Jed
and me reminds me of something that has happened between
God and me. Often I sense God's saying, "Stop right here, go
no further." Most of the time I stop, but sometimes I don't. I
make the wrong turn or end up somewhere I shouldn't be.
Someday Jed will learn to trust my leadership, just as I've had
to learn to trust God's wisdom and leadership in my life.

One of the big reasons our family lives on this farm is
so we can do things together. Of course being a writer I don't
have to commute to an urban office complex or factory five
days a week. When I was growing up in Connecticut about
the only thing that Dad and I could do together was take out
the garbage, and that's not something a father and son want
to do together. As a boy, how badly I had wanted to live
someplace else where Daddy and I could do things together,
naturally, instead of having to make up things to do. Going
on a family vacation once a year just didn't seem like enough
togetherness; besides, that was the whole family instead of
just him and me.

The pickup bounced along, me steering, and Jed
standing next to me, his hand on my shoulder. He looked out
the window, turning his small head from side to side, just like
I did. I looked up at a walnut tree and Jed looked up. When I
stopped the truck, hopped out, and walked toward our lower
pond, Jed didn't want me to help him out of the truck. He
wanted to hop out just like I did. He jumped, almost landed
on his feet, and sort of bounced off the ground. Without a
whimper he scrambled up and kept moving.

Jed grabbed my hand and the two of us walked together. I'd never imagined that holding the soft hand of a little boy could make me feel such love and security. I was
awed...Life would continue, we would grow older together,
doing so much, taking care of each other.

I looked at the bank of our spring-fed pond and wondered if it had eroded this past winter. Jed seemed to be won-

dering about something, too. His light brown hair was in tight curls, exactly the way Barbara's hair looked in her baby pictures. I always laughed to myself when we were with my folks because they would say over and over that our children looked just like my brothers and sisters. Then, when we were with Barbara's folks, they would say that Jed looked exactly like Barbara as a baby and that Rebekah favored Barbara now. And of course, everybody produced pictures to back their theories.

The sun went away. A rain shower was coming from the north side of the farm, and I found myself wishing that Jed would walk faster, as we headed back for the truck.

"Please, Daddy, slow for me," Jed said.

His little stocky legs could not move any faster and he was trying with all his might to keep up with his Daddy. I had been walking along with God for the last ten years. God had been so patient with me and my babyish ways. He'd been such an unrelenting, yet gentle teacher. He'd never dragged me somewhere I wasn't ready to go or expected something out of me I was not yet capable of. I slowed to a stroll.

The wind was blowing harder now, from the Lochridge's farm. I picked Jed up to hurry him back to the truck, but really it was an excuse to hug my boy. I loved him so much. Now safely back in the truck, he wanted to steer as we drove through the pasture, just like his big sister Rebekah did. The first time Jed tried to steer I had to hold on very tightly because he jerked the steering wheel to the right and left. But Jed didn't like my hand on the wheel with his; he wanted to steer all by himself. At first I was very frustrated that Jed couldn't steer as well as Rebekah could, especially when he tried to knock my hands off the wheel. I found myself thinking that I should just forget about letting Jed learn. Whenever I thought those kinds of thoughts, though, I usually reminded myself about what would have happened if God had given up on me as unteachable.

So I kept on working with Jed, trying to teach him how to steer. Days passed and each day Jed left my guiding hand on the wheel a bit longer and didn't jerk the steering wheel back and forth so much. One day he got the hang of how to steer his way through the field, staying out of the ruts, going around trees and rocks. The more he seemed to understand how to steer, the less he seemed to mind my hand of guidance. Not bad for a two year old.

As we drove toward the house Jed said, "Daddy, go dat way!"

"Why do you want to go that way?" It was so exciting that we could actually have a conversation.

"Puppies." He wanted to go over to where Lacey's dog-house was because she'd recently had a litter of pups. Lacey's our Alaskan Husky.

At the doghouse, Jed pointed to some dry grass, still dormant from winter. "Lie down, Daddy."

He liked for me to lie down and let the puppies climb all over me. For a week he'd been trying to work up the courage to lie down with me and try it. He picked up the biggest male, the one with the black streak down the middle of its nose and dropped him on my stomach. He thought this was hilarious and fell down laughing.

Then Jed got up, unsteady from so much laughing and fell on top of me and the puppies. The silly puppies began to howl like wolves, except no wolf ever had such a high voice. We lay in the late afternoon sun, just rolling around, having a blast.

Jed got up and all four pups waddled after him. He stopped and shouted, "Daddy. Ook *Ook!*" *Ook* meant "look." There was concern in his voice.

I walked over to see a dead squirrel lying in the grass. Lacey often brought food to her pups, just as mama wolves do.

"What's dat, Daddy?" He tried to pet the gray, furry animal.

"It's dead," I said without thinking that Jed had no idea what *dead* meant. How could I explain *dead* to a child who was pure life? Just the day before I'd held a stethoscope to the kids' hearts and let them hear the beating sounds. Then I'd tried to explain that the sound of our heart made us live. I'd felt kind of stupid, but I figured they had to start somewhere. Now Jed wanted to feel the squirrel's heart. I held his hand on its cold chest.

"Daddy, squirrel won't run away from puppies?" Only I could have understood his version of these words.

"No, son, it's dead."

"Dead, Daddy." Jed turned away and began walking toward the house. I wondered what, if anything, he was thinking. Death had not really become vividly personal to me until the last few years when in my early thirties I'd begun to experience the loss of friends and family. There was no way for Jed really to understand death, but I was glad he was beginning to learn about the "big" things of life now.

That night it was my turn to put the kids to bed and since Jed and I had run around so much and missed his nap I took him upstairs about an hour before his beloved sister. I tucked him in, making an extra trip downstairs for his green blanket. Then I gave him a stuffed bear, which he threw on the floor. He acted like he was too tough to have to sleep with a silly stuffed animal. Let Rebekah sleep with her unicorn but not him.

After he said his prayers, I stood up. But before I could turn around Jed said, "With me, Daddy." That meant he wanted me to lie down with him until he had fallen asleep. Sometimes I did this when he was upset, but he'd never asked me to lie down with him when he was in such a good mood.

I wanted to take a shower and finish a book I was reading about Tibet and was thinking of an excuse when he said again, "With me, Daddy." He put a lot of emphasis on *Daddy*.

"Okay, little man."

He moved over so I wouldn't try to lie on his side.

Every so often he would turn his head and look at me to make sure I had not slipped away. I felt so secure lying there with my little son, the two Jenkins boys, him and me, squeezed onto a child-sized bed. Soon he stopped turning to see if I was still there, as if he knew I would always be there ...just as I knew that my Father would always be there when I needed Him.

Jed's sleeping face was a reflection of peace...peace that is normal for a little child...peace that wasn't normal for me until I got right with my Father.

Behold, children are a heritage from the Lord,
The fruit of the womb is His reward.
Like arrows in the hand of a warrior,
So are the children of one's youth.
Happy is the man who has his quiver full of them.
                                                    Psalm 127:3–5

24

On a Ledge of Faith
Peter

I remember growing up saying childlike prayers before meals that went, "God is great, God is good, now I thank Him for our food. Amen." At night we'd always pray with our parents saying, "Now I lay me down to sleep, I pray the Lord my soul to keep. God bless Mommy and Daddy, Peter, Winky, Scott, Freddy, Betsy, and Abbi."

In my late teens I decided that prayer like that was overly simplistic and embarrassing, and I didn't believe in prayer anymore. Then, in my midtwenties, I accepted God and Jesus as my own, and suddenly I believed in prayer again. But I had no idea how it all worked, until I began praying according to what was inside my heart and not from repetition.

Nowadays, prayer is as natural to me as waking up. I often think about what God wants us to pray about. He probably doesn't want us to pray trivial prayers about what we want to order at the drive-in, or where we are going to park at the shopping center. I doubt He's really interested in hearing a prayer about whether or not our clothes that just

211

came back from the cleaners will stay clean through two wearings—even though He can keep track of all these details. When I first tried to comprehend this it completely blew my mind. How could anyone or anything keep track of so many specifics? But then I thought about the computer and how a big one can keep up with millions and probably billions of pieces of information.

When I first began learning about what a computer can do I felt a little insecure, thinking that maybe a big, mainframe computer could store more things in its memory than God could in His. It didn't take me long to realize this was a stupid thought since God was the one who gave man the intelligence to invent the computer in the first place. After all, we all know that the Lord allowed the computer to be invented so ministers could send out millions of form letters. Just kidding!

I believe that if God could give human beings the intelligence to invent the computer then His abilities are far beyond any computer's. That means that for Him to keep track of a trillion prayers is a piece of cake! Detailed prayers are *no problem!* He can easily keep track of trillions of pieces of information. In fact I'm sure the word *trillion* to God is about equal to a *thousand* to you and me. Think about all the things that He can remember, all the people He keeps track of, and yet He never gets bogged down with all the information and is still capable of loving everyone!

If God can know so much and have such easy and rapid access to all of it, then He can hear prayers that are really detailed. I believe the Lord wants us to pray finely tuned prayers about the really important things in our lives. He wants us to pray specifically about things that really matter, like whom we will marry, and where we should live. I think He wants us to ask His help in our careers and ministries and to ask His guidance with our children, families, and spiritual lives. He wants us to rely on Him.

One windy October night I was sitting in my favorite

reclining chair, enjoying that special time of the night when Barbara and I could just sit in the same room and talk without raising our voices. The children were asleep, which meant they weren't practicing mountain climbing on one of us or running through the room like a stampeding herd of buffaloes.

I could not get Mike and Gail Hyatt off my mind. The Hyatts were a young couple who had moved to Tennessee from a medium-sized city in Texas just a few weeks earlier. They knew no one in town other than Bob Wolgemuth, the president of the Nashville company that had hired Mike to be vice president of marketing and advertising. I'd met Mike once a year or two earlier in Texas in a conference room filled with people.

Even though I was reading a fascinating book about the first astronauts, *The Right Stuff,* I could not force the Hyatts out of my mind. I stopped reading and said, "Okay, God, are you trying to say something to me about these people?"

Then I remembered that they were seriously considering buying some land out in the country, away from the suburbs, as Barbara and I had done, even if it meant Mike would have a longer drive to work. I felt compelled to call them, even though I fought the thought. I wanted to suggest to them that they find a place to rent first, to see if they would like the country lifestyle. I knew from experience that many people who think they want to live in the country are caught up in the romance of it all. But after they step in a few cow patties or a bull breaks down their yard fence and eats the entire garden, then they decide it wasn't quite like their dream, after all.

So I picked up the phone and dialed the number at the condominium they were renting in a suburb. Gail answered and I asked to speak to Mike. He got on. His voice was filled with the energy and the enthusiasm that made him such a good marketing and advertising man.

"Mike, this is Peter Jenkins, how are you doing?"

"Hey!" Mike said, sounding pumped up, "I'm great, how about you?"

"Fine," I said, feeling like I was about to pry into someone's life. *Maybe I shouldn't say anything*, I thought. *No, I'd better!* Some of the greatest things I'd experienced with God had come when I'd just obeyed, even though I had stepped way out on a ledge of faith.

"Listen, Mike. I've got an idea for you. Would you mind hearing me out?" I still felt nervous, like my insides were about to shake.

"Go ahead," Mike said, sounding a bit wary.

"I don't know if you know it, but I grew up in the suburbs just as you and Gail did. All my life I'd wished that I could live out in the country." I paused, feeling better, like, just maybe, I was doing the right thing.

"Please forgive me for being bold, but I would suggest that you find yourselves a place to rent out in the country, just to find out if everyone in the family likes the lifestyle." There was a silence that seemed unusually long for Mike.

"What do you mean, Peter?" he finally said.

"Well, I've noticed that sometimes the husband loves living in the country and the wife hates it. Or the kids love it and the wife loves it, but the husband's too far from work or the golf course, or too close to his family. Or the wife can't stand being so far out in the 'wilderness.' " *There are so many reasons it could go wrong*, I thought. But, I didn't want to sound too negative.

"Oh really," Mike said, sounding as though he might be resenting my intrusion.

"Another problem is, Mike, that if you leap out and buy something and then don't like it, it's usually harder to sell rural property." I stopped to catch my breath. Mike said nothing. I fought off feeling like an idiot.

"Please forgive me for intruding but I just wanted to welcome you and your family to the area." I groaned inwardly. Often when I get excited I say the thing I most want to say first, when I should be saying something more socially polite like, "Welcome to Tennessee."

I plunged on. "By the way, if you would like to rent something, we have an empty house on our farm that we'd be glad to rent you for a while." *Now that sounds really bad. He may think you're just trying to rent him a house!* Mike didn't know that we had people coming out of the woodwork trying to rent the place since rental property was scarce in the country.

"I'd like to talk with Gail about it, Peter, and thanks for calling."

Had I jumped ahead of God or just *thought* He was compelling me to call the Hyatts? Normally, when my feelings were this strong I knew I was being motivated by the Lord. But this time could be way off base. Why did I put myself through such a debate every time I thought I was being prompted by God to do something?

The next day, just before the late night news came on TV, the phone rang. It was Mike.

"Peter, we've prayed about what you said last night and we'd like to take you up on your offer. Does it still stand?"

"Sure does! That will be ten thousand dollars a month rent! No, seriously, we'd be glad to have you as neighbors, and your two girls will have our threesome for playmates."

"Great. We'd like to come down this weekend and take a look at the house, if that's all right."

"How about Saturday afternoon?"

And that's how Mike and Gail and their two daughters, Megan and Mindy, came to be our next-door neighbors, or should I say "next-farm" neighbors.

What I didn't know was that Gail prayed very detailed prayers about the important matters in her family's life. One cold winter's night three months later, when the Hyatts were at our house for dinner, Gail said that she'd written down a week or so before my "awkward" phone call exactly the kind of place she felt the Lord wanted them to live in.

The prayer, written on yellow, lined notebook paper, went like this:

October 9, 1984: By Gail Hyatt.

Prayer request: My family and I live on a farm not too far from south Nashville. The land is absolutely beautiful and lends itself to after-supper strolls. The children have lots of fun places to explore and many trees to climb, and they especially like to play in the creek. Mike's favorite way to unwind after a hectic day at the office is to fish for bass in the pond out back. There are productive fruit trees, and we keep a garden growing.

The house is warm and cozy with lots of character. It is excellent for entertaining and housing guests. We use it a lot to minister to others and bring glory to the Lord. The farmhouse sits up on a hill, off the road, and has a beautiful winding driveway. We love living in the country and find it easy to fit into the lifestyle and the community.

Gail had read this prayer twice each day.

Well the good Lord heard Gail's prayer and compelled me to call. The place they're renting from us is exactly what she described in her prayer, except that the pond behind the house, where Mike's supposed to fish after a hectic day at the office, only has sunfish in it, not bass. I was planning to stock it with bass this next summer. Mike will still get to fish for bass, though, since the Hyatts are planning to be our neighbors until they find, or should I say, until God finds them some land and a new home. By then maybe the bass will be old enough to catch.

So Jesus answered and said to them, "Assuredly, I say to you, if you have faith and do not doubt, you will not only do what was done to the fig tree, but also if you say to this mountain, 'Be removed and be cast into the sea,' it will be done.

"And all things, whatever you ask in prayer, believing, you will receive."

Matthew 21:21–22

25

Beginning with the Ends of the Earth

Peter

U sually when I read the Bible I can think of something from my life that relates to what I'm reading. My favorite books in the Old Testament are Psalms and Proverbs. One winter night after Barbara and I had put the children to bed, I opened my Bible to the Psalms. I had both wood stoves fired up and the crackling heat attracted me to them. I curled up on a chair, with cracked vinyl covering, and began glancing through the Psalms. The first one I paused at, Psalm 61, had only come to life for me recently. It reads like this:

> Hear my cry, O God;
> Attend to my prayer.
> From the end of the earth I will cry
>   to You,
> When my heart is overwhelmed;
> Lead me to the rock that is higher
>   than I.

For You have been a shelter for me,
And a strong tower from the enemy.
I will abide in Your tabernacle
    forever;
I will trust in the shelter
    of Your wings.

Psalm 61

Not until I'd been to the ends of the earth would Psalm 61 mean much to me. Just a few months before I'd been in Lhasa, the biggest city in the most mountainous and isolated area in the world, Tibet. As I had stood in a crowded and dusty marketplace, I'd felt as if I had walked through a door in my house in Tennessee and stepped back a thousand years. I was surrounded by a mass of Tibetan people and the sharp smells of yak butter. Merchants nearby, who looked as though they'd never taken baths, were selling animal skins and deadly-looking daggers.

I was in Lhasa heading for the Himalayas and Mt. Everest, the earth's tallest mountain, towering more than twenty-nine thousand feet into the sky. I was part of a team planning to be the first Americans to reach the summit of Everest by a never-before-climbed route from the China side. Some of the men who were part of our team were unlike any men I'd ever known. Lou, Jim, Skip, Geo, Phil, and the others found normal living just too safe and comfortable. They went anywhere in the world, seeking out mountains that would test their extraordinary stamina and strength, always willing to risk death to prove that they could conquer these obstacles of jagged ice, heaving snow, and vertical rock. They wanted to squeeze the maximum out of their lives, and climbing mountains was the way they chose to do it.

In Tibet—on the most exotic adventure of my life—I felt powerfully homesick, a homesickness that overwhelmed my ability to appreciate where I was and what I was doing. Never had that happened to me while walking across America. Even though I now was with close friends I felt desperately lonely. I wanted to be home with Barbara, Rebekah, and Jed. I wanted to go for a ride in my Ford pickup on a summer's afternoon. I wanted to ride my Tennessee walking horse and smell freshly cut hay. I missed my homeland, the USA. I'd only been out of my country twice before, just over our borders, in Canada and Mexico. There was no TV, no radio, only the labored sounds we were all making trying to breathe at fourteen thousand feet.

Sundays meant nothing in Tibet, one of the world's most important centers of Buddhism. The Dalai Lama used to rule Tibet from "His Holiness's" 999-room Potala, the Buddhist's version of the Vatican. This was before the Chinese Communists had taken over and declared that Buddha was no longer to be worshiped. Before the violent takeover, every Tibetan family had been required to give one of their sons to become a Buddhist monk. Even after their leader, the Dalai Lama, fled for his life to India and the Chinese blew up their temples, the Buddhists had clung to their "god." Everywhere I went, the Tibetans, who looked like very weathered American Indians, walked down the dusty roads with their prayer wheels, chanted while working, and lay flat on their faces quoting holy words and reading scriptures.

I desperately missed our little country church back in Tennessee. I wanted so badly to shake hands with our caring congregation after one of our pastor's great sermons. Chunks of Homer's sermons came out of my memory, and I wished I could see him crossing our porch, just stopping by the house for a "tawk." But I was thirteen thousand miles away. Never had the desire for fellowship been so powerful in me. I pictured Rebekah in her frilly yellow Sunday dress, shiny black shoes, and white socks with lace trim on top, coming down the stairs so proud and clean and pretty. I could see Jed getting dirty the minute after Barbara had finished putting his clean clothes on him, combing his hair, and washing his face. The boy was so much like his daddy.

Something could have happened to them, halfway

around the world, and I wouldn't have known about it. Feeling so insecure was very unusual for me, and I had nowhere to turn but *my* God.

Walking through this other-worldly open-air market filled with items I'd never seen before, I felt almost deserted by God. My Bible was back in my dirt-floored room. I needed assurance and I needed it right now. I glanced down a narrow alley between two stone buildings that looked thousands of years old and saw two people walking away from me, a larger man and a smaller person about the size of Rebekah. The man reached over and put his arm around the thin Tibetan boy.

A Scripture I'd never needed before came to my mind. I didn't know it word for word but *here and now* it didn't matter: "Son, I am always with you, no matter where you go, even to the end of the world."

I knew He was here with me. He'd heard my cry and answered my prayer, even though I was calling to Him from the ends of the earth. He'd led me to the rock that was so much higher than I!

I kept reading through Psalms, but first I put another log on the fire. I recalled yesterday morning when I had driven my old tractor across the frozen grass as I did every winter morning, headed out to feed our cows. It felt good to feel the cold wind turning my cheeks red. When the cows heard my tractor they all came running from wherever they were on the farm, knowing I had a load of hay. This morning they were in a pasture behind the spring-fed pond. I wondered how the red fox pups were doing that had been born by the pond in a den of limestone rock.

I drove up a hill overlooking our farmhouse, threw out the hay, and sat there watching the hungry herd eat. I knew every cow and calf by their very distinctive personalities.

The sounds of someone driving up our long gravel

driveway attracted my attention, and I looked down to the farmhouse and saw Barbara pulling up in our pickup. The truck was loaded with all kinds of furniture. Today would be a day to remember for our family. And it would be a historic day for our farm, which rests among easy-rolling pastures of middle Tennessee. The time had come to move back home. For the year and a half we'd been restoring the farmhouse we had lived in town, in the old Parks home. That house had given us shelter from the winds, rain, snow, and summer heat, but not much more. When a strong wind blew, gusts inside the house would blow the corners of the rugs off the floor. Just a few days ago I had looked toward our Christmas tree and seen it shaking. Surely the wind wasn't that strong. Well, it wasn't the wind. Barbara had strung popcorn and woven it around the tree, and two mice were shaking the tree as they ate the popcorn.

The restoration of our farmhouse had begun at the foundation which was solid rock, native limestone. At times we had become frustrated by the slow progress of the restoration and for comfort and guidance we would read this Scripture from the Bible: Jesus said it, "Whoever comes to Me, and hears my sayings and does them, I will show you whom he is like: He is like a man building a house, who dug deep and laid the foundation on the rock. And when the flood arose, the stream beat vehemently against that house, and could not shake it, for it was founded on the rock" (Luke 6:47–48).

As important as the building of our house had been to us, our relationship with God had been far more important. We needed Him when life darkened toward hopelessness. We needed Him as much and maybe more when our life seemed almost perfect.

I came to Psalm 91. By this time Barbara was sitting on the sofa next to my chair.

"Listen to this, Barbara," I said.

He who dwells in the secret place of the Most High

Shall abide under the shadow of the Almighty.
I will say of the LORD, "He is my refuge and my fortress;
My God, in Him I will trust."

Surely He shall deliver you from the snare of the fowler
And from the perilous pestilence.
He shall cover you with His feathers,
And under His wings you shall take refuge;
His truth shall be your shield and buckler.
You shall not be afraid of the terror by night,
Nor of the arrow that flies by day,
Nor of the pestilence that walks in darkness,
Nor of the destruction that lays waste at noonday.

A thousand may fall at your side,
And ten thousand at your right hand;
But it shall not come near you.
Only with your eyes shall you look,
And see the reward of the wicked.

Because you have made the LORD, who is my refuge,
Even the Most High, your habitation.

"That's beautiful, Peter," Barbara said.

I felt such a profound sense of peace in our farmhouse as the wood fires kept the winter chill away and as God's book kept away the inner chill of my occasionally insecure soul.

Barbara was reading *Country Living* magazine. I thought I'd just let the Psalms keep falling open and read whatever my eyes focused on. Next came the fifth Psalm, the first three verses.

Give ear to my words, O LORD,
Consider my meditation.
Give heed to the voice of my cry,
My King and my God,
For to You I will pray.

Just the other day I'd been thinking about how much I pray. More often than not I'd pray while doing other things, as opposed to kneeling by the bed with the children or praying before a meal, which I did, too, but at those times I tended to be much less specific. I prayed my more detailed prayers while cutting firewood, feeding the horse, changing a diaper, driving to the airport, writing a chapter, or jogging a few miles. I was surprised by how many different kinds of things I prayed for, but I was more surprised by how natural it was to pray. I was always unconscious of my constant praying until I reflected back on just what I'd prayed for and seen God had answered.

I remembered back to the first jacket-piercing winds of that fall, the first warning that winter was near. When those winds hit Tennessee, I always climb up the ladder into the loft of my barn. There I sit on a bale of hay and reflect on the year.

One November day the hay had smelled especially sweet. I thought about all the times I'd prayed for that hay. When spring had come I had prayed for enough sun and rain to make the clover and grass grow. When late spring had changed to early summer I had asked God to make our rain soft and long, so that it would soak into the ground and not run off. When the grass had grown knee-high we had cut the hay and when the freshly cut hay had been ready to bale I had asked Him for a dry day, because rain could have ruined all our work. It hadn't rained that day or the next.

As I thought about all of this, a cold gust of wind blew in my face and I looked around the filled-to-overflowing barn. Every once in a while I feel a little silly praying for things like hay, but that has not stopped me from relying on Him. As I climbed down the ladder to head back home, I thanked God for helping me with the hay, and for so much more. I prayed for world peace and for our children. I prayed for my sister and my family back in Connecticut and Michigan. I prayed for God's direction in relation to my career, and

I prayed that my dogs wouldn't kill any more of the neighbor's chickens. Come to think of it, I prayed about everything.

The fire was dying down, and Barbara had already gone upstairs to get ready for bed. I could hear the branches from our maple trees hitting the tin roof and the occasional pop of a log as it burned. Before going upstairs I would have to go outside to the ice-encrusted wood pile and load up both stoves so that all of us would sleep warm and cozy, protected from the frigid north wind. As much as Jed kicked off his covers I knew I'd really have to get the stoves cranked up.

Before I went out to face the wind, ice, and cold, I read this:

> My soul, wait silently for God alone,
> For my expectation is from Him.
> He is my defense;
> I shall not be moved.
> In God is my salvation and my glory;
> The rock of my strength,
> And my refuge, is in God. Psalm 62:5–7

After putting two more armfuls of wood in our two woodstoves, I went to bed. I hadn't slept that soundly in a long time.

As newborn babies, desire the pure milk of the word, that you may grow thereby.

1 Peter 2:2

26

The Little Girl on a Windy Hill

We were on our way to pick strawberries on a fine spring day in May. Not too hot, a slight breeze, and the air alive with sweet smells of blooming flowers. Bumblebees buzzed. The sky was a summer blue with white puffs here and there, and the fields were emerald green. Many of our traveling friends who came to visit us said this part of Tennessee reminded them of the rolling hills of England, Wales, and Scotland. Someday, we'd go there with our family, but right now, Rebekah and Jed were too small and we were enjoying farm life too much to travel. There would be a time later for taking them on adventures across the world.

Rebekah, almost five, sat in the front seat with me as we drove down the country road to the berry patch. Our windows were down, and her chestnut-brown hair blew in her face.

"Mommy?"

Here comes another question, I thought. It seemed as

227

though I had become an answering machine.

"Mommy, how do flowers eat and drink?" she asked as she looked at the pastures of wildflowers.

"From the rain. They drink water from the rain and get their nourishment from the dirt. That's the way they eat." I felt proud of my answer. Simple but understandable.

"How does the rain eat?" Rebekah asked.

I struggled to answer. Just as I was about to explain where the rain comes from, how it forms, the cycle of heat and condensation, she changed the subject and started to ask another question. I was relieved.

"Mommy?" Rebekah was deep in thought.

"Yes, dear."

"Mommy. Babies don't have hair inside their noses do they?"

Rebekah Pennell Jenkins was our first experience at parenting. She had turned from a cooing baby into a curious, adventurous little girl, almost overnight. Here was this miniature person, a little lady, my daughter sitting next to me. I wondered if her curiosity came from just being a child, from her explorer father, or from her part in the walk across America. I had been almost two months pregnant with her when we splashed into the Pacific.

We parked the car near the owner's farmhouse, collected several quart boxes, and walked up the hillside to the strawberry patch. At least five acres of berries lay in front of us, secluded on the backside of this farm. No one else was here. Sometimes, people would come with friends and pick all day, but now Beka and I were the only ones here. Birds sang to us as we walked between the rows, looking for the right place to start picking. Rebekah jabbered, calling me to look here, look there, and hurry.

"Wow! Look here Mommy. Look how big this one is!" She popped the red berry, almost the size of a plum, into her mouth. I showed her how to pull the berries, gently, off the stems and drop them into the box. I explained how easily they would bruise, not to step on the plants, don't tip over the box, don't pull the whole stem off the plant, watch out for the bees, don't get too far ahead of me—and more.

"Mommy. I wish I were as big as you."

"Why, honey?"

"Then I could tell you what to do."

It was a precious day together, just the two of us, alone, on the windy hillside with the juicy berries. My feelings for Rebekah were as sweet as the berries. I adored my only daughter. She was like Peter in many ways. Her childish face was already pretty, but it was her free spirit, not her beauty, that turned my heart. She was so full of life, innocence, and personality. Secretly, I prayed that my darling daughter would be protected from her own talented, fanciful, and beautiful self, which could lead to problems if not channeled properly. I talked to God about her as I bent over the berries and asked for His guidance in raising my charm girl. A peace came over me, an inner quiet that matched the quietness on the hidden hillside.

The soft breeze kept us company. Soon Rebekah's shorts and shirt were streaked with red juice and a red stain circled her mouth.

"See, Mommy. See how many I have. Much more than you." She pushed her quart box under my nose. About a dozen berries were scattered on the bottom of her box, some half green, some too small.

"Yes, dear. I'm so proud of you."

"Mommy?" I ignored her. I wanted to pick at least eight quarts this morning.

"Mommy!"

"What Rebekah?" I was getting annoyed.

"Mommy, why is God three people?"

I thought a moment. I kept on picking the berries and shifted my position. My knees and back were getting sore.

"Well, there's God the Father, God the Son—that's Jesus—and God the Holy Ghost."

"What's the Holy Ghost?" she asked.

"That means the Holy Spirit; you can't see the Spirit, but you can feel Him like the breeze out here today."

"But, why is it called the Holy Ghost? Ghost? Is it scary?"

"Honey, back in the old days of the Bible, they just used the name Ghost instead of Spirit. It's not spooky or scary. Ghost and Spirit are the same. Holy Ghost is just an old-fashioned way of saying Holy Spirit."

"Oh." She thought a moment. "You mean real old-fashioned...sort of like 'Little House on the Prairie?' "

"Yes, dear. Sort of like that."

And Jesus called a little child to Him, set him in the midst of them, and said, "Assuredly, I say to you, unless you are converted and become as little children, you will by no means enter the kingdom of heaven."

Matthew 18:2–3

Amen!

27

A Deep Calm

Peter

B arbara was nowhere to be seen. I focused my eyes intently on the lake, scanning the jade green water that was so calming to my spirit. Then, far off, a half-mile or more, I saw a doll-sized figure moving so fast that it was mostly a blur. I could see black, thick hair blowing in the wind. It was Barbara, and I was amazed at how quickly she had mastered the jet ski.

A jet ski looks like a snowmobile but goes very fast on top of the water. If you believe what you see on television, jet skis are supposed to be ridden by surfers, California blonds under twenty-two or anyone who is young, deeply tanned, and incredibly sleek. Surely these jet skis are for the wild and risky, the young and crazy. Many of the commercials for sodas, tanning creams, certain brands of punch, and exotic vacation spots show these kinds of people on either jet skis or wind-surfing boards. So watching Barbara, a mother of three who reads her Bible daily, zipping across the lake amazed even me. On her first try she had jumped on the thing and stood up going about thirty miles an hour. I hadn't seen her having this much fun in a long time.

After a while Rebekah and Jed came and asked where Mommy was. I pointed out on the lake, and they were very impressed. They expected this kind of thing out of Daddy, but Mommy on a jet ski—that was a "big time wow" as far as they were concerned. Fact is, Rebekah thought that the people who make *Sesame Street* should bring their TV cameras and make a movie of her mommy. She and Jed pointed out Barbara every chance they got to anyone on the beach who would pay attention.

This powerfully relaxing, pure, and very deep lake reminded me of both Alaska and Norway. It seemed like a combination of both places. The wilderness look of the trees that grew down to the lake's edge gave it that Alaskan feel, and the lake had a gentleness that the Norwegian lake and fjord country seemed to possess.

One of the many things that set Center Hill Lake apart from Alaska and Norway was water so warm in the summer that it felt better than a bathtub and more soothing than the ocean. The forty- to fifty-mile lake had hundreds of hidden coves and seldom-seen waterfalls. No ocean I'd ever seen had such a gentle surface and such caressing waves. There was no threat in this water, only an invitation to its healing and calming qualities.

As far as I'm concerned, there's something special about dipping in a lake that's so deep and clean and chlorine-free. This lake was fed by magnificent waterfalls and the incessant dripping of fern-covered springs, their water filtered pure by the greenest mosses.

Barbara, Rebekah, Jed, and I were here for a long Fourth of July weekend with our friends and neighbors, Mike and Gail Hyatt and their two girls, Megan and Mindy, both under five. Gail had found out a few months earlier that she was pregnant with their third child, and like most pregnant women she was worried that her bathing suit wouldn't look right. But she had worried for nothing and our weekend was a big success.

During the past year Barbara and I had been under a lot of pressure. I'd spent a summer alone in China, and Barbara had given birth to Luke, our "surprise baby." For more than a year, while restoring our home, we had lived in a house that felt more like a barn. In addition to writing two books simultaneously, we'd been running our farm, delivering baby calves when need be, and burying the ones that froze to death during a record-setting cold winter. The pressures had seemed at times more than we could stand up under. Without our Lord at our side we probably would not have been able to handle it all.

We took turns speeding around the lake on the jet ski, feeling the warm summer winds stroke our faces as we explored the deep coves in the lake. Heavy vines hung from trees to the water's edge, and I told the children to watch for gorillas or Tarzan. They thought that was exciting and it kept their concentration on the lake and not on their favorite place—the pool at Four Seasons Resort where we were staying in an A-frame cabin.

When we did bring the kids to the pool, they jumped off the sides with their inflatable plastic rings that had pictures of Care Bears on them. Then they worked up a lot of courage and jumped off the side with nothing around them.

Even two-year-old Jed decided he had to jump off the side of the pool, but only into my arms. That would have been fun if he'd have done it five or maybe ten times, but he jumped and jumped and jumped—maybe a hundred times, maybe two hundred times. My arms grew numb from catching him. The older girls, Rebekah and Megan, jumped off the diving board, finally, but I had be treading water right beneath them so they could land partially in the water and mostly on my head. Those girls could knock a grown man out, especially Rebekah, who, after she jumped and hit me, wrapped her strong and long arms around my neck and cut most of the air off from my lungs.

That Saturday night, sunburned, hungry, and thirsty, we went to a catfish restaurant. The children ran from one video game machine to the other, and then begged for quarters to feed the juke box so they could play their favorite country tunes like "Mama He's Crazy" by the Judds.

We four "grown-ups" tried our best to act as immature as possible, making up silly and sick jokes. "Barbara," I'd say, "do you know what I hate?"

"What do you hate, Peter?"

"I hate it when you jet ski in the ocean and a Great White Shark swims up behind you and has a feeding frenzy on your body! I hate that."

Mike chimed in, saying in a wimpy voice, "Yeah, I really hate that, especially when the shark swallows all of you but your head and then swims under water so long you can't hold your breath anymore. And what's even worse is that you're bleeding so bad about a hundred other sharks come to see what all the blood's about and..."

"I really hate that, too," Gail added. We kept this going until we ran out of crazy things to say or we broke up in hysterical laughter.

The kids shot puzzled looks at us, like we should be sent to our rooms until we could settle down. We just had a blast the whole weekend, even having a terrific time driving home in our station wagon, all eight of us seeing who could count the most horses and cows and goats on their side of the road. We arrived back at the farm completely relaxed and rested.

When the next morning came and it was time to go to the office, I'd forgotten what work there was for me to do. And I was so happy and stressless that I didn't even care. Even at the office, the twelve- by sixty-foot white and green trailer behind Luther's Grocery store, I remained in that deep calm state that had come over me at the lake. I was in the mood to do little or nothing—maybe get on the phone and call some friends I'd been too busy to talk to lately...maybe read some of the magazines piled on my desk...maybe listen to my new Amy Grant album...

I was in such a good mood I thought about taking the whole town out for lunch, but there was no restaurant in our fine town of one thousand one hundred that could hold all of us. What a relief! Our two books were almost done, we were living in our newly refinished farm house, the cows were done with their birthing problems, and Rebekah had just blown her first bubble using peach-colored bubble gum. It was just one of those special times in life.

The phone rang. It was my brother Freddy from Connecticut. He began to tell me about the final plans for our family reunion later in the summer. I heard the other phone ring a few minutes later, and after Wally answered, I heard him walking down the narrow hall toward my office. He didn't wait for me to look up.

"Peter, get off the phone, something's wrong!" He said forcefully. "It's Barbara." Wally had never acted like this before. I hung up immediately, lunged into the other office, and picked up the other phone. Barbara sounded frantic.

"Peter," she said, breathing hard, "come home quick! Luke [our eight month old] has just had a seizure or something. He's totally limp! He seems to have a very high fever, and his eyes just rolled up inside his head as I was cooling him off with cold wash cloths."

What a shock. What a drastic switch. My mind ran full speed until I could think of what I should do and say to Barbara.

"I'm on my way home. You stay with Beka and Jed and I'll come get Luke and take him to Dr. Mishu's office. Call the doctor to let her know we're coming." This physician, who had an office right next to our trailer, had just recently moved to our town.

Thinking of Luke completely limp with his eyes rolled back in his head, maybe serously ill, I couldn't stand taking him to the doctor alone, so I asked Wally if he would come with me. We both burst out of the door and drove as fast as we could the mile or so to our farm.

I leaped out of my car and with a step or two was in the house. Barbara was hovering over Luke who lay on the kitchen counter, and he didn't seem to be moving.

"What's wrong with him?" I asked, trying to be somewhat calm in front of Rebekah and Jed, who were watching, wide-eyed.

"I don't know. I think he's running a high temperature, but I can't find our thermometer!"

"Has he been like this all day, so—so..." I started to say "lifeless," and then couldn't use the word. "So limp?"

"Yes, he's been very lethargic and sick, but he seems worse now."

I grabbed our little red-headed, blue-eyed Luke in my arms. He was our biggest baby yet. He was already twenty-five pounds at nine months and wore Jed's clothes. His head flopped to one side.

Gravel and hot dust flew everywhere as Wally and I sped down our driveway to the doctor's office. Dr. Mishu and her dark-haired assistant were pacing the floor, ready for Luke.

The doctor covered him in cool towels that looked like surgical cloths. She took his temperature. It was over 104 degrees, and that was after Barbara had been cooling him off in the sink for the past hour. Dr. Mishu felt the soft spot that was still on the top of his head. By this time Barbara had pulled up in her station wagon because she couldn't stand waiting at the house. There was an air of intense concern and unspoken thoughts of the most serious kind.

I took Jed and Rebekah to our office in case something really bad happened and in a few moments the phone rang. Barbara said that the doctor advised us to rush Luke to the emergency room at our county hospital, about twelve miles away. I ran next door, finding Luke still wrapped in those damp, throwaway towels. Dr. Mishu said in a hushed voice, "Peter, drive carefully. But please get there as fast as you can."

It didn't matter to me that this road to the hospital

was the biggest speed trap in middle Tennessee. I drove that Chevy station wagon as fast as it would go. I don't know how long the trip took, but it seemed like a day. The whole ride felt like slow motion—like a television replay of President Kennedy's assassination or a knockout in a boxing match.

Luke could not hold his head up; his skin was colorless and felt like fire; and his whole body was limp and loose. Barbara and I didn't say much but our minds whirled with similar thoughts. *Will Luke die before we get him to the hospital? Will he die there? Is he suffering brain damage right now from his extreme temperature? What else is going on inside his body that Dr. Mishu is so concerned about?*

I thought about what we would tell Rebekah and Jed if Luke did die. I tried to stop such thoughts but I couldn't. All of this had hit me by such surprise that up to this point I hadn't even thought about praying.

Prayer! My hand instinctively stretched toward Luke and I laid it on his chest, which now felt strangely cool. Barbara must have been thinking the same thing, we both began to pray for him at the same moment.

"Please God, help little Luke hang on till we get to the hospital. Fill him with Your life and help him, God." This had happened so fast there had been no time to alert our pastor. "God, let him live...Please, Lord."

Luke seemed to be getting weaker. I told Barbara to slap him, to see if that might make him more alert. It didn't. His head fell from side to side as Barbara tried to hold him up. Time dragged and other drivers seemed to be going nowhere and had forever to get there.

We ran up to the admitting entrance, and the electric door seemed to open at quarter speed. The waiting nurses rushed Luke and Barbara back into one of the emergency rooms. Dr. Mishu had called ahead, and everyone seemed very concerned. The young woman who was filling out the forms recognized me and wanted to talk about our books and find out when the next one was coming out. I had a hard time hearing her or remembering my address or anything else.

Dr. Thompson, one of our excellent pediatricians, arrived shortly after we did. I knew something had to be serious, because this doctor and his partners saw hundreds of kids each day at their busy practice.

Luke lay on a table covered with a white sheet. Three or four nurses huddled around Dr. Thompson and us. They drew blood, having a hard time finding a vein. They took his temperature. They did everything they could think of. Then Dr. Thompson decided to take some spinal fluid to make sure he didn't have spinal meningitis. The doctor and nurses wondered aloud if the soft spot on the top of his head was swollen.

After all of this testing Luke seemed about the same. We were asked to wait in a private room until the results of some of the tests came back. Dr. Thompson came in and talked to us. He told us all the things that could be wrong. He said that high fevers and seizures in children Luke's age were not uncommon. He didn't think that Luke had spinal meningitis, but he wanted to be ever so careful. He would know more when the blood and spinal fluid tests came back. For now, Barbara and Luke would have to check into the hospital for tests and observation, at least for the night.

I got them checked into room 326. Dr. Thompson reported soon after that there was no spinal meningitis, but he had found that the sodium level in Luke's blood was very low which could be affecting his body's ability to fight off fever, flu, and other diseases. After a day in the hospital on high sodium fluids, little "Lukey" became much more normal. After his second day, he was just about his usual little self.

After I had loaded Barbara and Luke into the car and we were headed home from the hospital, we talked about how close we'd felt to God during our ordeal. We were deeply thankful for medical science and our committed doctors. But we were most thankful that on wonderfully calm happy days by the lake, or during the agonizing moments while a child struggled to live, we could make it through because of the strength of our relationship with our faithful Lord.

On the same day, when evening had come, He said to them, "Let us cross over to the other side." Now when they had left the multitude, they took Him alone in the boat as He was. And other little boats were also with Him. And a great windstorm arose, and the waves beat into the boat, so that it was already filling. But He was in the stern, asleep on a pillow. And they awoke Him and said to Him, "Teacher, do You not care that we are perishing?" Then He arose and rebuked the wind, and said to the sea, "Peace, be still!" And the wind ceased and there was a great calm.

But He said to them, "Why are you so fearful? How is it that you have no faith?"

Mark 4:35–40

Good question!

Does the story you just read - change anything you believe? I'd like to know!

P.G.